# THE MAN HER LOVE BUILT

## A Memoir of Love, Loss, and Becoming Whole

### NOAH KAIROS

# Table of Content

*This story is based on true experiences. Some names and details were changed for privacy, but the lessons and emotions are real. This memoir is a tribute to the love and labour of a single mother, and an honest reflection on the process of defining manhood for myself.*

# Introduction

The journey of a thousand miles - they say - begins with a single step. They won't tell you, though, that as easy or reachable it may seem, you cannot take that step alone...

I guess I still remember how that step began for me. It was just another morning, much like the one we see every day; shades of the subtle sun, a clear sky and the daring determination to move out there and conquer the world. Mornings always gave new strength.

A faint glow of morning light slipped through the kitchen window as Mother flipped the last pancake onto a plate. I was twelve years old, slouched at the table in my wrinkled school uniform, still rubbing sleep from my eyes. The smell of syrup and butter mixed with the crisp autumn air sneaking in through a cracked window. Mother moved around the kitchen in a well-practiced dance of activity - packing my lunch with one hand while nudging my textbook toward me with the other.

"Eat up, and don't forget you have a math quiz today," she reminded, her tone firm but not unkind. I mumbled a yes with my mouth full of pancake, which earned me a gentle swat on the back of my head - a wordless mind your manners. She had a way of balancing warmth and strictness in a single action. One moment she'd be fussing over a stray lock of my hair that refused to lie flat, the next she'd arch an eyebrow and ask if I'd finished the homework, she saw me neglecting the night before.

As I shovelled in another bite, I watched her methodically tie the laces on my worn-out sneakers. Normally, a kid my age might feel embarrassed that his mom still tied his shoes, but I knew this morning ritual by heart: she did it not because I couldn't, *but because she wanted to make sure I started the day cared for in every possible way.* It was one of the countless little things she did to smooth the rough edges of our lives.

On the counter, her phone buzzed with a reminder for a parent-teacher meeting scheduled for that evening. She silenced it and jotted a note to herself on a sticky note which she proceeded to pin on the fridge whiteboard. She was desperate not to forget. Between her hospital shift and my school events, our calendar looked like a game of Tetris.

I remember when I had forwarded my teacher's mail to her. Of course, I couldn't ask her directly:

"Will your father be joining us?"

Mom hadn't answered that part; she never did. Instead, she'd forwarded it to me with a smiley emoji and a note:

*We'll be there.*

Just the two of us - as always.

I gulped down the last of my milk and grabbed my backpack. Mom handed me my lunch bag, pausing to tuck in the tag sticking out of my collar. "Remember what we talked about: if something feels tough today, do your best and don't be afraid to ask for help. Okay, honey?"

"Okay, Mom," I sighed in that drawn-out way preteens do, rolling my eyes for good measure. She responded by tweaking my nose, making me crack a reluctant smile. I realized she was doing it again - playing both good cop and bad cop, the comforter and the taskmaster. In that moment, her presence filled the kitchen completely. There was no gap she didn't try to cover, *no role she wouldn't slip into for my sake.*

As I headed out the door, she called after me, "Love you! Be good and be smart!" Her words were both an encouragement and a gentle command. I glanced back to see her standing in the doorway, a mug of coffee in hand, still in her scrubs from the night shift but smiling brightly through her exhaustion.

Walking down the block toward the school bus stop, I felt a familiar mix of emotions: pride that she was my mom and a small, quiet awareness that something was missing.

At twelve, I couldn't fully name it, but I felt it - like the hollow vacuum of a presence meant to be filled. Even so, I squared my shoulders. Mom had given me everything I needed for the day packed neatly in my bag and what I needed for my life tucked neatly in my heart.It struck me, even then, in a hazy way: her love was doing the work of two people. And somehow, that love made our little world feel whole, even when it was just the two of us.

# The Single Story

Mornings like these were a familiar routine, but I've come to realize not everyone saw our little two-person unit the way I did. And so, with time as I grew into life, I got to learn a phrase. It's called **the "single story."**

It was the idea that people sometimes have a single, simplistic narrative about a group of others, and they apply it to everyone in that group without thinking. For families like mine - a boy raised by a single mother - the single story often goes like this:

*He must be missing something essential. He's
bound to be troubled, or angry, or doomed to
struggle. In other words, his home is broken; his
father is not present...*

I encountered that story everywhere, even if it wasn't always said out loud. On TV, the kids without dads were often portrayed as lost souls or troublemakers, thanks to widespread misinterpretation pushed by the mainstream media. At school, well-meaning teachers offered extra sympathy I hadn't asked for, assuming I needed saving. There were the neighbours who gave Mother a sad smile every now and then, as if to say *poor you, doing it all alone.* And there were the occasional classmates who would blurt out questions like, "Don't you miss having a dad?" - the answer to which was complicated, more complicated than simple a yes or no.

The truth is, every family is different. My reality defied the easy label of "broken home." Yes, there was something - someone - missing, and that mattered. But there was also so much love and strength present that it kept our home standing strong. I wasn't some inevitable statistic, and Mom wasn't some tragic figure or saint; we were just a family, *with our own story.*

And so, with close thought and a strong resolve, I have chosen to share that one lived experience in full, in all its nuance.

I pour out my heart, not to argue that every single-parent household is perfect or that fathers don't matter nor to cast blame or spark some political debate about family structures.

All that matters here is the honesty, as raw, as soothing, as liberating it may be.

Because besides the stereotype and the single story; the assumptions that a boy like me was destined to be broken and angry - there were real people. There was my mother, there was me, and there was the life we built together. Our story won't speak for everyone, but it's one truth among many. And two truths can co-exist. Perhaps, if I tell it right, it will chip away at that single story and make some room for understanding.

Before we dive deeper, I'd love you to experience this story as my one-on-one conversation with you, sharing what I saw, felt, and learned. You should also know that while I'm definitely shaped by my background - I'm just an ordinary man from a working-class family, raised in a place not too different from lots of towns and cities you'd recognize - this story isn't about any one country or culture or people. I won't be focusing on the politics of where I grew up or the specifics of the neighbourhood beyond what's relevant to our personal journey.

The themes we'll explore are human ones: the need to belong, figuring out who you are, finding love and holding onto it, learning to be resilient when life gets tough. Those experiences aren't confined by geography or race. So even though my perspective is rooted in being the average son of a single mom, I hope readers from all walks of life will see something of themselves in these pages.

It's also important for me to say what this book is not. It's not a manual or a self-help guide that will give you "10 steps to succeed" or a lecture on how society should be. I'm not interested in preaching or handing out rules. Instead, think of this as part memoir, part reflection. I'll tell you about real moments from my life - some happy, some painful, many mundane but meaningful in hindsight - and then I'll share what I took away from those moments. If you find some wisdom or comfort in those reflections, I'll be grateful. And if something doesn't resonate with you, that's okay too. Take what's useful and feel free to leave the rest. This is a personal story, not a universal blueprint, and I respect that each reader will connect with it differently.

Because this story involves other people - especially my mother and father - I want to set some ground rules up front, mostly for myself. This is a tribute to my mom's labour and love, but I'm not going to put her on some impossible pedestal. Yes, in my eyes she was a hero, but she was also human. She got tired, she made mistakes, and she had her own dreams and frustrations. I want to honor her without pretending she was perfect or that she had to be perfect. Celebrating her work as a single mother doesn't mean I think single moms have to do it all or do it flawlessly. No parent does.

As for my father, you won't find any mud-slinging here. The fact is, he wasn't around when I was growing up, and that's a source of pain that will come through in these pages. But I'm not here to publicly shame him or to air every detail of what went wrong between my parents. Where I talk about him or the hurt of his absence, I'll do it honestly and, I hope, with respect.

A note on privacy: in writing this, I've changed or obscured a few names, dates, and identifying details. The core of every story is true, but I might blend together a couple of events or use a childhood nickname instead of a real name for someone. This is to protect people's privacy - my mom's, my father's, and even mine. The last thing I want is to cause anyone harm or embarrassment.

Finally, I can promise you that I will not sensationalize anything. There won't be shocking twists thrown in for drama's sake or any tragic detail milked just to pull at heartstrings. I'm also steering clear of any "culture war" narratives. This book isn't an argument for or against any social agenda. It's not about saying one kind of family is better than another. It's simply the story of how I grew up and what I learned. I'll keep it sincere, I'll keep it responsible, and above all, I'll keep it real.

## The Perfect Timing

You might wonder, why tell this story now? The truth is, I've carried it around for years, quietly. As a boy and as a teenager, I rarely talked about what it was like growing up without a dad around. Partly, I didn't have the words. Partly, I was afraid of being pitied or judged. I didn't want anyone's *"that poor kid"* sympathy, and I certainly didn't want to prove the people right who expected me to stumble. So I kept my head down and my feelings to myself.

But a few things changed as I entered adulthood. For one, my mom and I had a conversation not long ago that planted a seed. We were sitting at the kitchen table - me home on a rare weekend visit, her stirring sugar into my coffee like I was still that little boy who needed every kindness - and she said, almost out of the blue, "You know, you should consider sharing some of what you've been through. It might help someone."

At first, I shrugged it off. *My story?* I'm just one guy, nothing famous or sensational about me. But her words stuck.

Around the same time, I started mentoring a freshman at a local community college - a bright kid who reminded me a bit of myself at 18. One day he asked me, "How did you figure out how to be a man, growing up without a dad?" He asked it innocently, out of genuine curiosity, but I found myself momentarily speechless. That question lingered with me for days. How did I learn? How did I avoid some of the pitfalls everyone predicted for boys like me? I realized I had a lot to say in response - about my mom, about the men who did influence me in bits and pieces, about the lessons I learned the hard way.

And then there's the world we're in now. There are so many mixed messages about manhood floating around. Some say a man should always be tough, never show weakness.

Others say men need to get in touch with their emotions and unlearn old habits. I felt caught in the middle of those messages, shaped by a mother who taught me tenderness and strength in equal measure. It feels like a critical moment to add a personal voice to that conversation. Not to give a grand theory, but to offer an example of one way it can be - a way that owes a lot to a strong woman's influence.

In the end, I realized the cost of silence was that people like that college freshman - or their single moms - might feel alone in their experiences. If I kept everything I learned to myself, I'd be closing the door on an opportunity to support someone. By telling this story, I'm choosing to open that door. It's a bit scary, sure - putting your life on display always is - but if even one person finds reassurance or insight in these pages, it'll be worth it. For me personally, writing this is also a way to honor my mom while I have the chance and to make sense of my own journey one chapter at a time.

And now, is the perfect time.

# In Readiness to Dive

Let me give you a sense of what you'll find as you read on. Each chapter in this book is woven from two kinds of thread: story and reflection. I'll invite you into specific moments of my life - you'll be right there with me as I navigate a childhood memory, a tricky situation at school, a conversation that marked me deeply. These scenes will be told as vividly and honestly as I can manage, sometimes with humour, sometimes with raw emotion. It was all a rollercoaster experience back then; it will be right now as well. But I won't stop at just telling you what happened. After each story, or woven into it, I'll step back and reflect on what it meant in the bigger picture. I'll talk about what a particular experience taught me, how it shaped my thinking or my character, and maybe what it could mean for others in similar shoes.

Don't worry, this won't turn into a lecture. The reflections are there to illuminate the story, not to overshadow it. One chapter might illustrate how I learned to ask for help without feeling ashamed, and I'll reflect on how important that lesson was for a young boy trying to be "tough." Another chapter might show a time when Mom's gentle side and stern side both taught me what real strength looks like, and I'll talk about how that redefined manhood for me. There are lessons about gratitude, about vulnerability, about forgiveness - the kind of everyday wisdom that isn't flashy, but sure goes a long way in life.

I've tried to write all this in clear, down-to-earth language. You'll notice the chapters are divided into short sections. Life kind of happened in pieces - a scene here, a conversation there - and that's how I present it. That means you can read a section or two, pause and think or take a break if you need, and then come back without feeling lost. It's a book you can digest at your own pace.

## To the Audience

Now, who is this book for? I wrote it first for sons like me who were raised by single mothers - I want you to feel seen and understood, to know that some of the confusing mix of emotions you might have - love, gratitude, anger, longing - are all valid and shared. I also wrote it for the single mothers out there, as a way of *saying I see you, and thank you.*

Perhaps a mom might even share parts of this with her son, as a conversation starter or just a reassurance that others have walked this path. Beyond that, it's for friends, family members, teachers, mentors - anyone who cares about a young person from a home like mine and wants to understand a bit better what that experience can be like. And honestly, it's for anyone who enjoys a story of growth and wants to peek into a life that might be different from their own. I believe we all become a little better when we try to understand each other's journeys.

To help you navigate, here's a quick roadmap of the book:
- **Part I: Foundations** - These first chapters delve into my early years. I'll share what it was like in the beginning, when I first felt the gap left by my father's absence and, at the same time, the full weight of my mother's love. This part covers the fundamental lessons and experiences of childhood in a single-mother home: how I started learning about life from a woman who had to play both mom and dad, and the first flickers of confusion I felt about "being a man" without a man in the house to show me how.
- **Part II: The Journey** - The middle chapters follow me into adolescence and the turbulence of the schoolyard and teenage life. Here, you'll see how I navigated friendships and bullying, and sought out role models - some good, some not so good - to fill the void of a father figure. This is also where I began to understand the scope of Mom's sacrifices - seeing her work multiple jobs, experiencing moments where I desperately wanted to ease her burden. It's a period of trial and error, of testing boundaries, and of slowly realizing what kind of man I wanted to become.
- **Part III: Becoming** - In the final chapters of the story, I'm on the cusp of adulthood and then stepping into it. This part is about how I ultimately defined manhood for myself. It explores my first steps into love and relationships, and how being raised by Mom influenced the way I treat partners and handle emotions. It also focuses on the theme of gratitude - how looking back, I've come to see gratitude as one of the strongest pillars my mother quietly built in me, giving me stability and perspective as I face the adult world on my own terms.

Throughout the book, I aim to keep the tone warm, honest, and down-to-earth. I'm not going to hide what hurt - when something was painful, I'll say so plainly. But I'll also be gentle and compassionate, both to my younger self and to the others in these stories. The language you'll read is straightforward; not big words to dazzle you or poetic flourishes to overwhelm you. That said, I do love the little details of life - the smell of my mom's coffee, the sound of her keys in the door, the way my heart pounded at certain moments - and I'll include those sensory touches so you can be there with me. I promise to avoid drowning you in overly purple prose.

I do hope the story stays relatable. I want you to feel like you're walking alongside us, not being preached at. It will all be plainspoken, warm, direct; a quiet memoir offamily and passion you will never forget.

Come, let me tell you the story of Mother, the woman that raised a man without a father!

PART

1

# Foundations

**"Take the first step in faith. You don't have to see the whole staircase, just take the first step."**
*- Martin Luther King Jr.*

# CHAPTER 1

# THE ABSENCE & THE PRESENCE

It's early evening and the smell of garlic and tomatoes drifts through our small living room. I'm seven years old, sprawled on the rug with crayons and a worksheet of spelling words I'm supposed to be practicing. From the kitchen, I can hear Mom humming softly as she stirs a pot on the stove. The tune is something she picked up from the radio - cheerful and warm - and it blends with the sizzle of onions in a way that makes the whole house feel cozy.

"Have you finished those words, baby?" Mom calls out, her voice raised just enough to carry over the simmering dinner.

"Almost!" I shout back, though in truth I've been doodling superheroes in the margin for the last ten minutes. A moment later, her face appears around the doorway, eyebrow arched - she has a sixth sense for when my attention wanders. Caught, I stick out my tongue playfully and earn a gentle headshake in return.

She disappears again, and I hear the clank of a pot lid being set aside. I turn back to my worksheet and make a real effort this time, whispering the letters under my breath: "B-R-A-V-E, brave... H-O-N-E-S-T, honest..." These words feel big and important. Brave. Honest. They're the kind of words Mom uses when she tells me what she hopes I'll grow up to be.

A few minutes later, Mom calls me into the kitchen. Dinner is almost ready - spaghetti tonight, a weekly staple - and it's my job to set the table. I hop up and grab the plastic plates from the cupboard. There are only two of us, but I take out three plates by habit.
For a split second I'm not even sure why I did - it's just something I started doing whenever I set the table, an unspoken curiosity if maybe one day there'd be a need for that extra plate. My hand hovers over it. Mom is watching me now, and a gentle understanding passes between us. Without a word, I put the third plate back and carry twoplates over to our little dining nook.

Mom comes over with the pot of spaghetti and sauce, and I can see the tiny frown line on her forehead that appears whenever she thinks I might be feeling that empty space. But just as quickly, she smiles. "Extra hungry tonight, were you?" she teases, nodding at the plates to brush off the moment. I shrug, and she ruffles my hair.

We sit down to eat, just the two of us at our small wooden table pushed up against the wall. There's an empty chair on the other side that we never use; it's become a convenient spot to drape laundry or park my school bag. Still, sometimes I glance at that chair and imagine someone else sitting there. Not a clear face - just a shape, a presence that's never materialized.

The sounds of our forks and spoons clinking are the loudest things in the room for a bit. Mom asks about my day, and I tell her about the art project we started in class and how I got paint on my uniform again. She feigns exasperation, covering her eyes dramatically with one hand. "What am I going to do with you, Picasso?" she laughs, and I giggle into my milk.

We talk about the spelling words and how brave and honest are not just words for tests but qualities she already sees in me. "You know, you were very brave last week when you stood up for your friend on the playground," she mentions. My cheeks warm at the praise. Then she adds, "And honest, too, when you told me the truth about what happened, even though you thought you'd get in trouble."

Her voice is filled with pride and it lights me up inside. Moments like this, I feel like I'm the center of the universe because she makes it so. Her eyes are on me, listening, encouraging, scolding when needed, but always there. In those instants, the absence of anyone else fades away and our tiny home feels completely full.

After dinner, I help her wash up. I'm on drying duty (a job that mostly means I'm stacking cups in wobbly towers until she rescues them). We make a game of it - she passes me a wet dish and counts "One Mississippi, two Mississippi" until I manage to swipe it dry and we both cheer when I beat her countdown. Soap bubbles catch the light as I laugh. Mom has a way of turning even chores into something fun or at least bearable.

When we finish, nighttime has settled in. Mom checks the locks on the front door like she does every evening, and I notice she pauses a second longer, staring at the bolt. I wonder if she's thinking what I sometimes think - that it's just us, and if something went bump in the night, there's no man of the house to check it out. The thought passes like a shadow.
She clicks the lights off in the kitchen, leaving just the soft yellow glow of the lamp in the living room.

"Time for homework check," she announces, back to business. I groan dramat-

ically, flopping onto the couch with my notebook, and she laughs as she sits beside me. The cushion sinks under her weight, and she puts an arm around my shoulders, scanning my wobbly letters and doodles. I brace for a scolding about the sketches, but instead she just traces one of my superhero drawings with her finger and says, "Nice muscles on this one."
We share a grin.

In that moment, with her arm warm and steady around me, I feel completely safe. The world outside our door might have all sorts of things we lack - money, a bigger family, a dad in that empty chair - but inside our home, we have everything we need. It's a world made of two people, doing their best, and for a child basking in his mother's love, it feels like two worlds at once: one full and one with a quiet, persistent gap. I lean into her and let that fullness wash over me, content for now in the haven she's created.

## The Father's Day That Belonged to Mom

In first grade, our class made Father's Day cards out of construction paper and glitter. I remember sitting at a tiny desk, tongue sticking out in concentration as I drew a lopsided heart and the words "Happy Father's Day" in shaky letters. Our teacher, Ms. Reed, walked around praising our artwork, and when she stopped by my desk, I could feel her hesitate for just a second.

*She knows*, I thought. I had never met my father and certainly wasn't going to see him that Sunday. I wasn't even sure "Father" was a word that truly applied to me. Ms. Reed recovered quickly and put a hand on my shoulder.

"That's beautiful," she said softly. "You can give it to someone who takes care of you, okay?" I nodded, pretending not to notice the pity in her eyes. That afternoon, I marched home with the card clutched in my hand and gave it straight to Mom.

"Thank you, baby," she said, her voice thick with emotion as she pulled me into a hug. I remember how tight she held me - it was like she was apologizing without words, even though it wasn't her fault. I hugged her back just as hard, wanting to comfort her in return.

As I grew a bit older, the questions started coming, sometimes from others, sometimes from inside my own head. When I was about nine, I was at a friend's birthday party at the park. All the dads were huddled by the grill, laughing and flipping burgers, while the moms chased little siblings around. My friend's father tossed him in the air and caught
him, both of them squealing with delight. I laughed along, but a strange feeling gnawed at me. It wasn't jealousy exactly - I didn't know what having a dad felt

like to even be jealous of it - but more a growing awareness that I was... different. One of the other boys, a kid known for speaking before thinking, asked me point-blank,

"How come your dad never comes to anything?"

There was no malice in his voice, just pure curiosity. Still, I felt heat rush to my face. I shrugged and mumbled something like "It's just me and my mom," and quickly pretended I had to help with something to escape the conversation.

That night I asked Mom, for maybe the second or third time in my life, about my father.
"Where is he?" I whispered while she was tucking me into bed. For years she'd kept her answers simple: "He lives far away," or "He's not with us, but you have me." This time, perhaps because I was older, she sat on the edge of my bed and sighed. In the dim glow of my nightlight, I could see a sadness in her eyes that mirrored what I felt in my chest.

"Your dad loves you, in his own way," she began slowly. "But sometimes grown-ups... they have problems or responsibilities that make it hard for them to stay. It's never because of the kid. It's never because of you. Do you understand?" I nodded, though I didn't really understand. Not why a person would leave their family, anyway. But I understood she was trying to tell me I wasn't to blame. She kissed my forehead and added, "You can ask me anything, anytime, okay? I know it's confusing."

Confusing was an understatement. What started as a quiet curiosity in child-hood quickly sharpened into a phantom ache by the time I hit middle school. It felt like an invisible missing limb - most days I forgot it wasn't there, but the world had a way of poking at the wound until it throbbed. I felt the difference acutely: staring at the blank line on my sixthgrade family tree, or bracing against the pitying glances of well-meaning adults who suggested my mom "must need a break." Quiet curiosity gave way to embarrassment, defensiveness, and a sim-mering anger I didn't know how to place. The absence was no longer a concept; it was personal, it hurt, and I carried it like a hole in the page, still too young to articulate the faint, constant question: Why isn't he here?

## When Her Love Filled the Empty Chair

If my father's absence was a void, my mother's presence was the thing that kept that void from swallowing us. She was everywhere in my life, filling every role that needed filling. By turns, she could be the gentle caregiver who kissed scraped knees and the strict enforcer who would accept no backtalk. As a kid, I sometimes thought she had superpowers - how else could one person do so much?

Take discipline, for example. One summer afternoon when I was about twelve, I decided it would be a brilliant idea to sneak out with a friend and ride our bikes far beyond the neighbourhood limits Mom had set. I felt a rare thrill of rebellion pedalling fast down a distant street, wind in my face, until I got home and found Mom pacing the living room with a look of pure panic-turned-anger. I'll never forget how her voice shook - not with weakness but with intensity - as she said, "Don't you ever scare me like that again." She grounded me for two weeks straight. No bikes, no video games, no hanging out after school. I fumed in my room that first night, thinking it was so unfair. Other kids had dads who might've just clapped them on the back for being adventurous, I told myself bitterly (whether or not that was true, I had no idea, but it fed my indignation). I even muttered under my breath, "You're too strict," loud enough for her to hear as I sulked behind my closed door.

A day or two later, the punishment still firmly in place, Mom knocked on my door. I braced for another lecture, but instead she sat on the edge of my bed. She looked tired - I noticed dark circles under her eyes that I hadn't before, probably because she hadn't slept well thinking of all the what-ifs of my little stunt. In a calm, soft voice, she explained that her rules weren't there to ruin my fun, but to keep me safe.

"When you didn't come home on time, I was afraid something happened to you," she said, and I saw tears glistening before she blinked them away. That hit me hard. I'd been so busy thinking about how I felt that I hadn't considered what I'd put her through. In that moment, I understood that her strictness came from love. She was being both mother and father in that situation - the one to lay down the law and the one to talk me through the feelings afterward. I apologized, my voice barely above a whisper, and she pulled me into a hug.

"I worry because I love you," she murmured into my hair. By the time my two-week grounding was up, I'd had a lot of time to reflect, and I came out of it with a new respect for the boundaries she set.

## Guardian Angel

Her nurturing side was just as impactful, often coming out in the quieter moments. I recall one night in middle school when I came down with a nasty flu. I was clammy and miserable, my head throbbing, nose like a leaky faucet. Mom had just finished a long shift at the hospital, and I could see the exhaustion in how she dragged her feet. Still, when she realized I was sick, she switched into full-on caregiver mode without a second's hesitation. She bundled me in blankets, brought me soup, and placed a cool hand on my forehead to check for fever every hour. Late into the night, I woke up groggy and disoriented to find her sitting in a chair by my bed, softly humming that same radio tune she liked, a damp washcloth in her hand ready to dab my face if I stirred.

"Mom, you should sleep," I croaked out. She just shushed me gently, saying, "A good mom's never off duty, sweetheart. You go back to sleep." Her figure was silhouetted by the hallway light, and I remember thinking she looked like an angel sitting guard. By morning, her eyes were heavy and red. She was only human, after all. Still, she got up to make me toast and tea. I recovered in a few days; she caught the flu right after and still went to work. When I think of dedication, I think of that night - her weary form next to me, refusing to rest until I was out of the woods.

Mom also did her best to make sure I didn't miss out on the typical "dad" activities. I could tell some things didn't come naturally to her, but that never stopped her from trying. When I joined the school's little league baseball team, she was out in the backyard with me on weekends, tossing balls in an old mitt for me to practice my swing. She threw like... well, like someone who had never played much baseball, with a hesitant, awkward lob. One time I smacked a line drive right into her shin. I panicked as she yelped in pain, dropping the mitt to clutch her leg. But she waved me off when I ran over, concern all over my face.

"I'm okay, I'm okay!" she insisted, even as a bruise started blooming. Then she put the mitt back on and forced a grin. "Show me that homerun hit again, champ." I realized then that she wasn't just doing it for me; she was also proving something to herself - that she could handle both roles, no matter what. Seeing her out there, limping slightly yet determined to keep pitching, is one of those images of my childhood that will forever stay with me. It's funny because at the time I found it a little embarrassing - I knew other boys practiced with their dads who actually knew the sport - but looking back, I'm proud. My mom had the guts to step into any role for me, even if it meant taking a baseball to the leg and swallowing her own pain.

## True Heroism

If you asked me back then to list the ways my mom was amazing, I might have pointed to the big, obvious things: how she worked long hours, or how she always showed up for my games. But looking back now, I realize the true heroism was often tucked into the quiet, small moments - the ones so ordinary I barely noticed them at the time.

I think of all the nights Mom was both exhausted and unwell, yet still present. One memory stands out: a stormy winter night when I was about ten. I woke up to a loud crash of thunder, heart pounding, convinced that the world was ending (as ten-year-olds often do during thunderstorms). Without hesitation, Mom scooted into my bed with me. She wrapped me in her arms and started talking in that soothing voice of hers about anything and everything to take my mind off the storm - pointing out shapes in the lightning flashes on the wall, telling me a funny story about how I used to chase rainbows as a toddler. I fell asleep to the sound of her voice and the steady rub of her hand on my back. Only later did I find out she had a fever that night. She'd felt it coming on at dinnertime but hadn't said a word, not wanting me to worry. I slept like a baby; she went to work the next morning, fever and all. At ten, I didn't grasp the enormity of that kind of sacrifice. But as an adult, I marvel at it.

*It's one thing to show up when it's easy - it's another to show up when every bone in your body is begging you to rest. A person who truly cares about you shows up nevertheless.*

Then there were the everyday inventions that at the time just felt like part of our family routine. Like "breakfast-for-dinner Fridays." I loved Fridays because Mom would whip up pancakes or omelettes in the evening, and we'd sit in our pyjamas and eat while watching a silly sitcom on TV. It felt like a whimsical treat, a break from the usual. Only years later did I connect the dots: Fridays were the end of the week, often the tightest stretch before her paycheck came in. Cooking breakfast food at night wasn't just fun - it was cheap. Eggs, flour, a bit of milk - she could make a filling meal out of almost nothing. I never knew we were scraping the bottom of the barrel those nights; I just thought my mom was the coolest for letting me drench pancakes in syrup for dinner. Realizing the intention behind that tradition still puts a lump in my throat. She protected me so well from the weight of our financial reality, turning what could have been moments of stress into memories of laughter and sticky maple syrup smiles.

Mom's quiet labour of love was woven into so many small details. Every Sunday evening, she'd sit down with my school uniform and inspect it for loose buttons or fraying seams. I remember lying on the couch, half-watching some nature documentary, while the lamplight caught the tiny glint of her needle. If she found a tear in my trousers, out came the sewing kit. Snip, stitch, tie it off - good as new. I rarely gave it a second thought; by Monday morning, my clothes were always ready and pressed. I certainly never considered what it took for her to learn those mending skills. It turns out she taught herself by watching videos on an old laptop, because hiring a tailor or buying new uniforms was money we didn't have. What I saw as just "Mom being Mom" was in fact resourcefulness and pride - she refused to let me go to school looking anything other than prepared, even if it meant sacrificing her limited free time on the one day she didn't work.

Even our tiny apartment bore the marks of her quiet strength. The cabinet door that always fell off its hinge? She fixed it with a screwdriver and sheer will, grumbling at the hardware but triumphant when it finally stayed put. The old clunker of a car that often threatened not to start? She'd be out in the cold with jumper cables at dawn, determined to get me to school on time and herself to work. She never waited around for someone else to solve a problem. If something needed doing, she figured it out or made do. And I absorbed that mindset without even realizing it.

At the time, I rarely thanked her for these little things. How do you thank someone for making your life feel normal and safe? As a kid, you just take it as a given. I expected pancakes on Friday and found my mended clothes on the chair and thought nothing of it. It was only much later, standing in my own apartment far from home, that the realization hit me like a wave: those "small" moments were anything but small. They were the infrastructure of love that propped up my entire childhood. The older I get, the more those memories shine. Not with the flashy brightness of big gestures, but with a steady, golden glow of a thousand quiet acts of devotion.

That's the paradox of presence, I suppose.

A hand on your back during a thunderstorm. Pancakes when the wallet is light. A neatly patched pair of pants. None of it makes headlines; there were no witnesses or applause. But those moments taught me the most about what love really looks like. It's not always dramatic or loud. More often, it's the patient, persistent care that happens when no one else is around to see. Mom never proclaimed, "Look how much I'm doing for you." She just did it, quietly, consistently. And in doing so, she showed me what strength really means: carrying on, caring on, in the small hours and the small ways that add up to something truly enormous.

## The Ignorance of Age

Of course, in the moment, I didn't always show appreciation. There were times I snapped at her or complained. If she forgot to sign a permission slip because she was juggling too many things, I might moan about it. If she made me do laundry on Saturday mornings while my friends were out playing, I'd grumble that she was working me too hard. Once, in a particularly nasty teenage mood, I even shouted, "You're not my dad!" during an argument about house rules. The silence that followed that outburst was crushing. I immediately regretted it, seeing the hurt flicker in her eyes before she gathered herself and simply replied, "You're right. I'm not. But I'm doing the best I can for you." I wanted to sink through the floorboards. How could she not have lashed out at me for that? Instead, she let the words hang, and later that night we talked it through. I apologized through tears, and she just held me, saying, "I know you didn't mean it. I know it's hard, baby."

Only later did I fully grasp just how much she balanced on a daily basis. She was the sole breadwinner, meticulously stretching every dollar from her paycheck to cover our rent, groceries, and my school supplies. I'd catch her at the kitchen table late at night, bills spread out, a pencil tucked in her hair, muttering numbers under her breath as she tried to make the math work. Yet, by morning, she'd be upbeat, packing my lunch with a note inside that said "Have a great day!" or showing up to cheer me on at my spelling bee during her coffee break. The woman never missed a parent-teacher conference, never missed a single one of my school performances or games if she could help it. I'd scan the audience, and there she'd be: still in uniform sometimes, a proud smile on her face, clapping louder than anyone.

In every way that counted, my mother showed up. She showed up when I succeeded and when I failed, when I was delightful and when I was a little monster. There was a constancy to her presence that acted like a counterweight to everything we lacked. Yes, she was only one person, but she made our family feel whole. Her presence was so overwhelming, in fact, that it often overshadowed the emptiness; it's only in hindsight that I see how deliberately she worked to make that true. At the time, I just knew that Mom was always there - the safety net that never let me hit the ground, no matter how hard I fell or how high I flew.

All those years, I lived with two emotions that pulled me in opposite directions: a deep gratitude for everything I had, and an equally deep longing for what I didn't. I was profoundly thankful for my mother - how could I not be? Yet, there was an ache I couldn't ignore, a wish that bubbled up in unguarded moments:

*If only I had a dad, too.*

The feeling often hit hardest in public, like during the seventh-grade soccer finals when I stood alone with Mom amidst pairs of beaming parents. I was grateful she was there, yet I couldn't help but imagine a father's arm completing the picture.

## Everywhere; Nowhere

Then there were times when even my ever-present Mom couldn't defy the laws of physics and be everywhere at once. She tried her best never to miss a thing, but life doesn't always cooperate. In eighth grade, I landed a small role in the school play. I was nervous and excited; Mom had traded a shift so she could come to the evening performance. But that afternoon, an emergency at the hospital meant she had to stay late. I didn't get the message until after the curtain call, when I checked my phone backstage. There was a text: *I'm so sorry, honey. Stuck at work. I'll make it up to you, I promise. Break a leg tonight - I know you'll be amazing. I love you.* Reading it, I swallowed a lump in my throat and blinked back hot tears. During the play, I had scanned the audience, twice, hoping to catch a glimpse of her familiar face. When I didn't see her, I told myself it was just the stage lights in my eyes. After the show, other kids were running up to bouquets of flowers and hugs. I drifted in the crowd, telling everyone that my mom had to work, trying to sound casual. They were kind - a friend's dad clapped me on the back and said I did a great job - but it wasn't the same. I biked home slow that night. When I walked in, Mom was waiting with an apologetic smile and my favourite ice cream. "I'm so sorry I missed it," she said, pulling me into a hug before I could even take off my helmet. I had planned to be tough about it, but the hug broke me.

I started to cry, mumbling, "It's okay, I get it," even though it wasn't entirely okay. She held me tighter and whispered, "Thank you for understanding." That made me cry harder, because a part of me hadn't understood at all - a part of me had been a hurt little kid, angry that the one person I counted on to always be there, wasn't there this time.

*My rational mind got it... But another part of me... didn't care about rationality. That part just felt the loss.*

The truth, which took me years to accept, is that it wasn't about "enough" or "not enough." I had an abundance of love, but I also had a real loss. *Those two things coexisted.* Loving my mom and appreciating her never cancelled out the question mark hovering over my life. And feeling that ache for a father didn't mean I loved Mom any less. I think both of us had to learn that. She once admitted to me, years later, that she worried she wasn't enough for me - that no matter what she did, she could never be a father. I told her the only thing that wasn't enough was the situation, not her. What she gave me was beyond enough; it was everything she had. But the absence was a reality too, one neither of us could completely fill.

Living with fullness and emptiness at the same time was confusing. I was at once richly blessed and quietly grieving. It's a strange thing for a kid to carry gratitude and grief together, not knowing how to make sense of it. On the outside, I played the role of the well-adjusted, happy kid - and genuinely, I often was happy. But inside, there were days I'd switch between joy and sadness so fast it gave me emotional whiplash. One minute I'd be laughing with Mom over dinner, truly content, and the next I'd be in my room listening to the muffled sounds of our neighbours - a dad's voice calling his kids to come inside - and I'd feel a hollow pang.

How did I come to terms with this?

*I learned to hold these two feelings in either hand,*
*like balancing stones. Over time, they taught me*
*empathy, I think – to recognize that people can*
*have conflicting feelings and that's okay.*

But back then, it mostly just felt like a quiet, private battle I fought inside myself: the battle between being thankful for what I had and yearning for what I did not.

Beyond our two-person household, there was a wider circle of people and voices that, for better or worse, shaped how I viewed my family situation. My mother might have been doing the work of two, but that didn't mean it was literally just us against the world - not all the time, anyway. We had some help, some supporters, and also our share of critics, gawkers, and well-intentioned meddlers.

My maternal grandparents were a quiet blessing in my life. They lived a couple of hours away, but we visited on holidays and some summers I'd stay with them for a week. Grandpa would take me fishing at a nearby lake, showing me how to hook a worm and cast a line. Those afternoons in a rickety boat, with him patiently untangling my messedup fishing lines, were some of the few times I got a taste of what a father-son outing might be like. He wasn't my father, of course, but he was a steady male presence, and I soaked it up. One Christmas, when I was around thirteen, Grandpa pulled me aside and gave me my first razor and shaving cream. I didn't have much more than peach fuzz on my chin, but he said, "Figure you should learn, for when the time comes." He taught me right there in the bathroom, lathering up and showing me how not to cut my face to ribbons. I remember catching a glimpse of my mom watching from the hallway, a soft smile on her face, maybe relieved that *someone* was there to guide me through that rite of passage.

We also had a couple of neighbours who stepped into our lives in little ways that mattered more than they probably knew. Mr. Jenkins, who lived next door, noticed when I was about eleven that I had taken a liking to basketball. He was a retired coach with grown kids, and on weekend mornings he'd invite me to shoot hoops in the driveway. He taught me how to do a layup and practiced free throws with me, his gravelly voice calling out encouragements like, "Eyes on the rim, not on the ball!" Those driveway drills became a regular thing. Mom would sometimes watch from the kitchen window, and I think seeing me laugh with an older man, even for an hour, gave her a sense of comfort - like the community was helping to fill in a bit of the gap.

But not all community attention felt good. Alongside care and comfort, came whispers and the pitying glances. Like the time one of Mom's friends from work came over for coffee and, thinking I was out of earshot, said, "I don't know how you do it alone. Boys are so hard without a father to keep them in line." Mom ushered me out of the room when she realized I'd heard, but the words lingered. Keep them in line - as if I were some wild animal that required a tamer, and my gentle, strong mother couldn't possibly manage it. Mom was livid later; I remember her apologizing to me for the comment and making it clear she didn't agree one bit. Still, it planted a seed of doubt in me:

*Was I going to be "hard to handle" as I grew up just because I had no dad at home?*

Society had a way of reminding us that we were deviating from the norm. I learned the phrase "broken home" around the same time I learned long division. It's a harsh term, casting judgement with just two words. I recall flipping through a magazine at the dentist's office and reading an article that talked about "children from broken homes" as an at-risk group for all sorts of troubles - poor grades, behavioural issues, future poverty, even crime. The checklist of negative outcomes made my stomach tighten. I was doing fine in school, I was well-behaved for the most part, but there I was, apparently one step away from becoming a statistic just because of my family structure. I glanced up and saw Mom in the waiting room, filling out my patient form, writing "N/A" in the section for father's information. In that moment, I felt a flush of defiance. How could anyone look at us and call our home "broken"? We had our challenges, sure, but broken? No. I snapped the magazine shut and tossed it aside, wishing I could do the same with those kinds of assumptions.

Even some professionals and authority figures carried that bias. In eighth grade, after I got into a scuffle with a kid who'd been picking on a younger student, I was sent to the school counsellor. I remember sitting in her pastel office, staring at a poster about selfesteem on the wall, as she gently probed about my life.

"Things at home okay? Must be tough without a father figure around," she said, pen hovering over her notepad. There it was - the easy explanation for why I might have gotten into a fight (never mind that I was defending someone else). I bristled and muttered that home was fine. She offered me a pamphlet about a mentorship program, suggesting it "might be nice to talk to a man every once in a while." I took it from her, but I never signed up. Walking home, I felt angry - not at her, really, because I knew she meant well - but at the assumption that I was automatically deficient or headed for trouble just because my family didn't fit the traditional mould.

For every person who thought we were a problem to be solved, there were others who lifted us up. An elderly lady from our church always made a point to tell my mother what a polite young man I was, adding, "You're doing such a wonderful job with him." Sometimes I noticed a hint of surprise in those compliments, as if they expected a single mom's kid to be unruly or lacking manners, but I chose to take the praise at face value. Mom certainly did - I'd see the pride in her eyes, and it was a welcome counterbalance to the negativity.

Community can do two things: it can soften the edges of a hardship, or it can make them cut deeper. In our case, we experienced both.

Over time, I gravitated towards those who reinforced the truth I felt - that my mom and I were a whole family, not a broken one. And I tried (not always successfully) to shake off the insinuations that I was doomed to be less-than because of the man who wasn't there. If absence had a chorus of naysayers, presence had a quiet choir of supporters, and I tried my best to hear the latter over the former.

If I had to distill everything from those early years into one lesson, it would be that absence shaped while presence saved. My father's absence undeniably left a mark on me - it drew the outline of a void that I would spend years coming to terms with. But my mother's presence filled that outline with so much love and support that the void never became the whole picture of my life.

That's the lesson of this chapter of my life: Yes, I grew up under the shadow of something missing, but I also grew up in the light of something profoundly present. And when all was said and done, it's that light - not the shadow - that made me who I am.

With that understanding of absence and presence laid down, I could finally see my childhood for what it was: not a broken tale, but a complex one threaded with both longing and love.

That was the first truth of my life.

# CHAPTER 2

# A WOMAN'S LESSONS FOR A BOY

I was standing in a grocery store parking lot on a sweltering afternoon when my car refused to start. The engine clicked and sputtered, but wouldn't turn over. A friend from work, who had been shopping with me, scratched his head and muttered something about the battery. He looked at me expectantly, as if I should know what to do. Without hesitation, I popped open the hood and pulled out a set of jumper cables I kept coiled next to the spare tire. The red and black clamps glinted in the sunlight as I hooked them up, just like I'd done many times before. Within minutes, I had the cables attached to a kind stranger's battery and my own. I told my friend to rev the donor engine. Sure enough, my car sprang back to life with a noisy rumble.

My friend slammed my hood shut for me and gave an impressed laugh. "Man, who taught you to jumpstart a car? Your dad must've made sure you knew cars," he remarked, wiping sweat from his brow.

I paused for a moment, feeling a familiar, bittersweet twist in my chest. I pictured my mother's determined face the day she taught me this very skill. I remembered how she'd dragged me out to the driveway one Saturday, an old car battery and cables on the ground, determined to prepare me for the kind of emergencies my father wasn't there to handle. I smiled at my friend. "Actually, it was my mom," I said quietly.

He raised his eyebrows in surprise. There was no time to delve into the whole story right then, but as I climbed into the driver's seat, the memory of my mother's voice came flooding back: "*Watch carefully, baby. One day you might be on your own and need to do this.*" At the time, I was just a kid, more interested in riding my bike than listening to car maintenance lessons. But she was right - I did need it one day. And that day, like so many others, I silently thanked my mother for teaching me something most people assumed a father would teach his son.

Driving home, I realized that most of my early life lessons - from tying a tie to handling schoolyard fights, from budgeting for groceries to coping with heartache - came from a woman rather than a man. Every step of the way, it was her voice guiding me. Growing up as a boy without a father in the house, I learned how to become a man in the embrace of a woman. The foundation of the man

I would become was built on my mother's lessons: each taught with warmth, firmness, love, and occasionally that tough edge she had to develop from playing both roles.

I found myself sorting through these memories like old photographs - Mom teaching me at the kitchen table, in the grocery store aisles, always determined to raise me right. By the time I pulled into my driveway, I sat in the quiet, realizing I was never truly without a teacher, only a different one than the world expected.

Believe me when I tell you that I was more than convinced that the path to manhood had to be carved out by a man's hands, steady and sure. To what extent could a woman be a progenitor of a real man? The question weighed on me. *It's much easier to associate the women with the young girls. Let them tie their shawls or wrappers, spend much time in the kitchen and learn what it takes to build a home.* I sigh quietly at this and wonder, "to what extent has the society chosen to misinterpret the role of a woman in the making of a child - a male child?"

My life lessons, unfortunately for the ever-scrutinizing, judgemental eyes of the society, came wrapped in an apron or carried in the lull of a good-night song. It took me longer than I'd like to admit to recognize that most of the truths I hold were spoken, or shown, by a woman - my mother - whose love quietly shaped me into who I am.

## Lesson 1 - You Break It, You Fix It

The summer I was ten, my world was our little neighbourhood - a sleepy street lined with low fences and watchful windows. One lazy afternoon, I was out in the front yard with a couple of friends, passing a scuffed soccer ball back and forth. The sun beat down on the pavement, making the air wobble with heat. We'd been told countless times to take our games to the park down the road, but of course, being ten-year-old boys, we thought this time nothing bad would happen.

I remember the exact moment trouble struck. I kicked the soccer ball, trying to arc it to my friend Kevin. But my aim was off - horribly off. The black-and-white ball sailed past Kevin's outstretched foot and crashed straight into our neighbour Mrs. Candice's front window. The glass shattered with a cringe worthy crash, loud enough to send a flock of resting pigeons exploding off a nearby roof. My heart leapt into my throat. In an instant, the carefree afternoon turned into a nightmare.

For a second, my friends and I just stood there in stunned silence.
"Run!" Kevin hissed, eyes wide. He took off down the street, and our other friend

followed. I was left standing alone on the lawn, knees locked in fear. Part of me wanted to run and hide too - maybe no one would know it was us. Maybe the adults would think a bird or a freak gust of wind did it. But before I could decide, I heard our screen door slam open.

There was my mother, attracted by the noise, stepping onto our porch with alarm in her eyes. She wore yellow dishwashing gloves and held a half-wet plate - she must've been in the middle of scrubbing dishes. Her gaze travelled from me to the broken window next door, and the puzzle pieces clicked. I watched her expression change from confusion to furious understanding.

My feet felt rooted to the spot as she marched across our yard towards me. "What happened?" she demanded, voice unnervingly calm but with a steely undercurrent. I flinched; I almost wished she would yell, because her quiet, firm tone was somehow scarier.

I stammered, "I-I'm sorry... I didn't mean to! We were just playing and... and I kicked it too hard - "

Before I could finish, old Mrs. Candice burst out her front door, her face red and pinched. "Who's responsible for this?" she shouted, pointing at the dangling shards of glass in the frame. She spotted me and narrowed her eyes. I was the only kid in sight - the obvious culprit.

I wanted to shrink into the ground. My mother quickly placed herself partially in front of me, a subtle gesture of protection, but I could see by her stance that I was not off the hook. "It was my son who broke your window, ma'am," Mom said, steady and respectful. "I'm so sorry. We will make this right."

Mrs. Candice huffed, clearly upset. "That window's been there twenty years! You kids..." she started, but my mother cut in gently, "I understand you're angry. I would be too. Let's talk about how to fix it." Her composed tone seemed to dis-arm the older woman a little.

Mom turned to me, and I braced myself. Her eyes were sharp. "Tell Mrs. Candice what happened, and apologize," she instructed firmly.

My voice came out a meek whisper. "I'm really sorry, Mrs. Candice. I was play-ing soccer and I shouldn't have been doing that here. I... I broke your window by accident." My bottom lip trembled, and I fought the urge to cry. Ten years old or not, I knew tears wouldn't get me out of this - not with my mom watching.

Mrs. Candice folded her arms. "Accident or not, someone has to pay for this," she grumbled.

"Yes, of course," my mother replied. Then - to my surprise - she placed a hand on my shoulder and said, "James will pay to replace the glass, out of his own pocket." I gaped at my mom. I didn't have any money, aside from the jar of allowance and chore money I'd been saving for a new skateboard. Hearing her words, I realized with a sinking feeling exactly where that money was going to go now.

"And until it's fixed," Mom continued, "he'll come over to help you clean up and do any other chores you need so you're not inconvenienced." Now my jaw nearly hit the floor. I could barely process that my mother was volunteering me for cleanup duty. Visions of spending my Saturdays pulling weeds in Mrs. Candice's flowerbeds or scrubbing her porch swirled unpleasantly in my mind.

Mrs. Candice pursed her lips, considering. Finally, she gave a curt nod. "Alright. I'll get an estimate for the repair. Make sure that boy shows up tomorrow to pick up this broken glass." With that, she turned and went back inside, closing her door with a firm thud.

As soon as she was gone, I started babbling to my mother in panic. "Mom, I don't have enough money for a window! That's... that's my skateboard money! And what if it costs more? Are you gonna have to...

"Mom held up a hand, silencing me. "Enough." Her voice was stern. "You were playing where you knew you shouldn't. You broke it, you fix it. End of story." She didn't yell, but her words brooked no argument.

Tears of frustration burned in my eyes. "It was an accident," I mumbled.

She sighed, kneeling down so she could look me in the eye. Her face had softened slightly, though her brow was still creased in disappointment. "I know it was. But accidents have consequences, James. Running away from them - or trying to blame someone else - that just makes things worse. You're responsible for what you do, even when it's not on purpose."

I sniffled and looked down at my sneakers, kicking at a tuft of grass. I felt miserable - for losing my skateboard savings, for having to face an angry neighbour, for letting Mom down. But deep down, I knew she was right. If I'd run off like Kevin, I'd still be responsible, and Mom would have found out anyway. A small part of me was actually relieved everything was out in the open now, even if the outcome stung.

That evening, after the summer sun had set, my mother helped me carefully pick every shard of glass out of Mrs. Candice's flowerbeds. I wore thick gardening gloves and carried a trash bag, while Mom held a flashlight steady. I kept expecting a lecture, but Mom just quietly worked alongside me. It wasn't until we finished and headed home, my shoulders slumped with exhaustion and guilt, that she finally put an arm around my shoulders. "I'm proud of you for owning up today," she said softly. "It wasn't easy, I know."

I glanced up at her in surprise. Proud? I had felt like nothing but a disappointment all day. She must have seen the doubt on my face, because she gave me a small squeeze. "Doing the right thing isn't always painless, baby. But it is the right thing. Remember that."

The window repair cost every dollar I had saved, and I spent two Saturdays repainting Mrs. Candice's front fence as a "bonus" apology. It was hot, tedious work. Yet, over those days, something unexpected happened: Mrs. Candice cooled down. By the second Saturday, she brought out lemonade and actually thanked me for helping. I realized she wasn't a monster, just a lonely elderly lady with a beloved home she worried about. In a strange way, cleaning up my mess not only fixed her window - it earned me her respect.

## Lesson 2 - Kindness at a Price

But I also learnt later on that this empathy, sometimes, came at a price. It so happened when I was ten and walked beside my mother through an alley behind our little apartment building on another cool evening. In the distance, I heard whimpers. Around the corner lay a scene I won't forget: a ragged boy, no older than me, sat on broken pavement. His knees were grazed and hands trembling. My mother bent down and spoke softly to him in such calmness that for a split second, I felt the split attention awkward.

"Are you hurt, sweetheart?" she asked gently. He wasn't, and we both knew it. "Where are your parents?"

Obviously, for some reason, they were not around. He was weak and starving, but he was alone. Mom took off her coat and laid it around his shoulders.

"Come home with us," she told him. That was getting creepy for me and awkwardness became insecurity, and trust me, I wasn't going to buy the "there's-always-space-for more" fantasy story.

Instead of turning away, we carried him home like he was part of our little caravan and I didn't like the idea. Mom read my discomfort all over me, but she was too engrossed in making the stranger feel okay. Inside our small kitchen, the first thing Mom did was set a bowl of hot soup before him. She nudged bread across to his plate and sat him on the sofa, checking his scraped knees with a gentle hand. Then she talked to him softly while he ate. He told us his father and mother had lost him in the traffic and when Mom requested to call any number she could, he mentioned not having their numbers.

She resolved to call the police instead and the boy became all panicky, much like he didn't like the idea. Mom felt it was just okay for little kids to despise the idea of the cops but for me, I just felt he wasn't so cool with his story - maybe it was my childhood instinct, meeting someone my age or I was just clouded by my own irritation with the entire situation. Whichever it was, Mom read my biases as being arrogant and as the child fell asleep on our sofa, she taught me that night to listen closely when others speak pain without words and of course, judgement. After he fell asleep wrapped in a borrowed quilt on our living room sofa, I sat with Mom at the kitchen table and we did the dishes together quietly.

She said, "You know, honey, he reminded me of you at that age - hungry, scared, looking for help. Sometimes when I see someone hurting, I try to treat them like I would treat you. You and he... you're not that different."

In the silence, I wondered what a father might have done. Definitely made a stronger resolve, not let emotions cloud his feelings to the extent that a total stranger sleeps on our couch. Maybe he would have turned the boy away or told him to fend for himself. Maybe he would teach me to be strong by ignoring pleas for help, claiming that "the world is hard, boy" just like I saw in the movies most times. But my mother showed me the opposite. She taught by example to step into another's shoes, no matter who that other might be. Her interpretation was uniquely strange as I have come to realize.

That night I lay awake thinking about the way the boy and how my mother's kindness had made his world a little brighter. But that only lasted a little while. It was when loud knocks came at our house the next day that we realized something was most definitely wrong. Apparently, some residents from a neighboring community had been out searching for the boy and as they crossed by area, a neighbour had reported seeing me and Mom walk home with the child. It was chaos unleashed. The family of this child were a swarm of aggressive mule, instantly accusing Mom of kidnapping their child when, evidently, the young boy was just waking up from sleep. The boy was reluctant about going home and later revealed he had actually run away from home and lied to Mom to have a place to lay his head.

Typical.

I was right and God, I wanted to scream it out at Mom that I tried to tell her it was a mistake. All that kindness and for what? She was almost tagged a kidnapper and the police had to step in. Good thing her identity as a nurse and the general public's knowledge of her works of compassion were there to stand in for her. But after it all, the family of the boy never saw the runaway child as a product of their deficient home and instead, they leaned into blaming the one who tried to save a child. It was when I made my point clear to Mom after the long brawl and we were both alone in the house that the lesson hit me hardest. After my entire rants of just how suspicious I was of everything, Mom looked at me, smiled and said: "I have no regrets, son." Those few words were about to change my life forever.

Kindness came at a price and the kind pay that price all their lives for nothing in return!

## Lesson 3 - Dirty Dishes, Clean Lessons

I remember a quick one; one where Mom turned my serious chores into a life lesson. The kitchen was our chapel and the midnight oil our communion. Everyone comes up with that stereotype that growing up with a single mother will tilt a man towards kitchen work. Yes, you're all right. It will! I must have been eight when I first stood on a wobbly stool by the sink with a rag in hand, helping my mother scrub greasy plates after a Sunday dinner. The lightbulb above us cast a warm yellow halo as the noise of running water and distant crickets kept time. My small hands trembled as I held a plate and soapy bubbles tickled my fingers. She stood beside me, humming a lullaby from her childhood, her eyes gentle but firm.

"Don't rush," she chided softly when I was about to toss a plate onto the drying rack. "Slow down and be careful."

I felt the weight of her words, heavier than the dish in my hands. With every plate I cleaned, she told me a family story tied to the meal we'd eaten - grandma's recipe for stew that came from generations past, the story of my first birthday cake last year. She made even soap suds seem sacred.

Later, I would wonder what a father might have done. Maybe he would have barked to get the job done faster, or done it himself in silence with frustration under his breath. Perhaps he would have said that a job worth doing was a job done without complaint. Mom, though, washed away complaint with kindness and detail. She explained that taking care of the dishes was like taking care of life's little messes: one scrub at a time.

By the time the last cup was clean and drying, I stood a little taller. I didn't know it then, but in that golden light, when the dishwashing became a ritual, I learned responsibility not through scolding or force, but through patience and purpose. Our mother-son chore time became a quiet covenant: I would grow up tending to life's duties, and she would help me see their meaning.

Even when I was a bit older, the routine in the kitchen continued. By age twelve

I was carving my path through the steam of summer dinners and the chill of winter mornings.

I remember one evening after football practice, coming home hungry to a table set but no one waiting. Mom had a gentle frown. "You missed dinner," she said without reproach. I shuffled in, and she swept me up to do dishes together. Our aprons matched; she teased that we looked like two chefs in a small bistro.

As we rinsed and stacked plates, Mom asked about my day - my new math lesson, my friends, the new girl on the bus. In the moment of working together, I didn't feel punished at all. In fact, I felt proud: I was growing into someone who cared for our home. I guess that's just one unfathomable talent of being able to balance a punishment and blessing such that both syncs equally well, you can't tell which is which.

I remember other mornings when I'd hear kids kicking and stomping about chores at their houses, where it was always a command from Dad or an older brother; I never heard a shout from my mom. Instead, I heard her turn up the radio while tending the garden or cooking. She made taking care of our home feel more like a contribution than an obligation.

By then I understood the way she treated those dishes - as if we were washing away the day together and starting fresh. A father might have assigned chores with a strict voice, likewise a mother; but in this case, we had a mother and father fused into one person and so the balance was achieved. She made sure I saw why those pots, plates, even socks mattered.

# Lesson 4 - Bending Without Breaking

Back then, the winter season back in those days came with a lot of preps. On one of such winter moments, though, when the winter crept into our kitchen through the cracks of the old window, hope crept out the back door. There had been some local government clashes earlier and some workers were quietly laid off - including Mom, leaving us with a hollow in our lives and our savings nearly spent. That evening I found her sitting at the kitchen table, lit only by the flicker of one small lamp. Her tired eyes reflected that dim glow, puffy from silent tears and the strain of holding it all together.

"Will we be okay?" I asked quietly, touching her hand with my small fingers.

Mom managed a weak smile that trembled at the edges. "We'll figure it out, love. We always do."

Next morning, a Tuesday, dawned grey and heavy. Instead of collapsing into despair, my mother did what she always did at six a.m.: she woke me gently, made breakfast, and kissed my forehead as I scrambled eggs at the stove with her guidance. The house smelled nice and felt warm, as if nothing had changed in the world except the layers of quiet worry in her eyes.

She put on her thick winter coat, kissed me on the cheek, and walked me to school in the frigid air, the snow crunching under her boots. "Remember," she said quietly, "a willow bends in the wind and never breaks. So will we." Her arms around me for a moment felt like a shield against the frostbite of fear. I could tell she was easily thinking out loud.

That night, we did homework at the table together. My pen paused, and I sighed over a math problem too hard for my tired brain. Mom put a hand on my shoulder. "It's okay to struggle," she said. "The struggle is like wind; it might bend us, but it doesn't have to break us. We just have to keep going."

As I worked on equations with her patient guidance, I felt a peculiar kind of strength grow. My mother wasn't a tall oak, rigid and unyielding, but a willow - graceful under pressure. She counted each small victory: each solved problem, each extra hour she put into job searching, each minute we lived by...

Some nights after, I would lie awake listening to my mother on the phone, negotiating job leads for someone she barely knew. The streetlights had long gone out, and the only sound was her soft voice as she made call after call, promising to show up at interviews even at dawn. I envied her ability to sleep on so little, to keep going no matter what.

Weeks later, I remember waking up to find a new worn-out jacket hanging on the doorframe. She whispered from the bedroom, "I start a new job today." It was a new hospital. She looked at me through the mirror with a sleepy smile and said, "You worry less about me, okay?" I nodded, feeling proud. It hit me then that she cared more about easing my worry than her own exhaustion.

I learned over time that setbacks were not the end of the road, but a detour around our next lesson. When I failed a test or didn't make the team, I often felt like we were falling back into the dark kitchen. Each time, though, Mom came around with words as warm as hot chocolate, encouraging me to try again in the light.

*"A willow may bend, but it also bends back,"* she would say, tapping my book with a finger. And little by little, I learned to stand up again.

# Lesson 5 - Get Back on the Bike

An interesting one - really. When I was about seven years old, my mother decided it was time for me to learn how to ride a bicycle without training wheels. I had a bright red bike that I loved, complete with a little bell and those rattling training wheels on either side. One Saturday morning, Mom announced it was the day to take them off. I remember feeling a jolt of excitement followed by pure terror at that idea.

We wheeled my bike out to the empty church parking lot down the street. It was early enough that the lot was deserted, the asphalt still wet with dew. I wore my favourite superhero t-shirt and a new pair of knee pads that Mom had bought for the occasion. She wasn't taking any chances with my safety.

My heart pounded as Mom used a wrench to remove the training wheels. Each twist of the bolt made me more anxious. *What if I fell? What if I cracked my head open?* I'd seen older kids zooming around on two wheels, making it look easy, but I felt wobbly even imagining it.

Mom must have sensed my fear because before I even got on, she knelt in front of me and adjusted my helmet strap snug under my chin. "I've got you," she assured, looking me in the eyes. "I'll hold on until you're steady. You're not going to be alone, okay?"

I nodded, swallowing hard. With that, I climbed onto the bike. My legs were trembling so much I could barely find the pedals. Mom stood behind me, both hands gripping the back of my seat and the handlebar. "Alright, take a deep breath," she said. "Now start pedalling.
I won't let go until I know you've got it."

I took one shaky pedal forward, then another. Mom jogged alongside, holding me upright. The bike wobbled wildly, but true to her word, she held me firm. "Keep going, keep the pedals moving!" she encouraged, a smile in her voice. I managed to circle half the lot like that; Mom practically bent in half running behind me to keep me balanced.

"Okay, I'm going to let go for just a second, James," she said after a few tries. "Just to see if you can balance. I'm right here."

"No - no, don't let go!" I yelped in panic, feeling the bike teeter.

But she already had, just for a heartbeat. For that single instant, I was riding on my own. I felt the freedom of it - the bike gliding under me, my hands steering without her support. A grin broke out on my face... just before I overcorrected, and the front wheel twisted sharply. Before I knew it, I was crashing hard onto my side.

The scrape of pavement on my knee and elbow burned hot. I hit the ground with a thud and immediately burst into tears, more from shock than pain. Mom was at my side in an instant. "Oh, baby, are you okay?" She helped me sit up and gently inspected my skinned knee, now oozing a bit of blood despite the knee pad which had slid off.

"It h-hurts," I hiccuped, tears streaming. I was embarrassed too - embarrassed that I fell so fast, that I was crying, that maybe I wasn't cut out for this.

Mom dug a tissue from her pocket and dabbed at my tears and the scrape. "I know it does," she cooed softly, giving me a quick hug. We sat there for a few minutes, me sniffling against her shoulder in the middle of the empty parking lot. I fully expected her to say we'd had enough and it was time to go home.

Instead, after I'd calmed down, Mom tilted my chin up. "Do you want to try again after we clean this up?" she asked gently.

I was incredulous. "Again? But I fell!" My voice was shaky and incredulous, as if falling once was proof I couldn't do it.

She gave me an understanding smile. "Falling is part of learning, James. You are doing it - you rode on your own for a moment there before you tipped. That's how everyone learns. They fall, and then they get back on."

I looked at my bike, lying on its side, handlebars askew. The idea of getting back on was terrifying. My knee was stinging and my confidence was shattered. I frowned, feeling angry at the bike, at the pavement, at myself. "What if I just can't do it?" I muttered.

Mom brushed some dirt off my elbow. "Can't do it yet," she corrected. "You're not a quitter. Remember when you first tried to tie your shoes? You got frustrated because it kept coming undone. But you kept trying every morning, and after a while you could do it with your eyes closed."

I shrugged, still unsure. She stood up and offered me her hand. "Come on, let's take a little break, get a Band-Aid on that knee, and try one more time. Just one more, and if it still doesn't work, we'll pack it up for today. Deal?"

I took her hand and nodded faintly. "Deal."

After a trip home for a Band-Aid and a juice box (and a stern talking-to I overheard her giving herself for letting me fall so hard), we returned to the lot. This time, I was determined not to let the bike beat me. Mom held on again and I started pedalling. My knee throbbed a little, but I gritted my teeth. We went back and forth, practicing balance. Each time she let go, I wobbled a bit less.

Finally, during one attempt, I realized she had let go and her footsteps had slowed behind me. I was doing it - I was actually riding on my own. I whooped in surprise. As for Mom, her laughter echoed across the parking lot.

In my excitement, I promptly lost focus and veered, but this time I managed to put my foot down and catch myself before I could crash land. I was breathless and exhilarated. The look of pride on my mother's face as she ran up and hugged me tightly is something I'll never forget. I think I grew two inches in that moment, bursting with pride myself.

That afternoon, I rode in wobbly circles until I was exhausted and the sun was high. Each time I fell, I got up a little faster. By the time we headed home (with me triumphantly walking my bike beside Mom), I had learned far more than how to balance on two wheels, though, like many other lessons in this chapter, I did not realize it then.

In that parking lot, Mom taught me the meaning of resilience: when you fall, you dust yourself off and try again. Ever since, whenever life knocks me down, I remember that little boy in the superhero t-shirt, and I hear my mom's voice: *Get back on the bike*, James.

And I do.

## Lesson 6 - Birds and Bees

No teenage boy ever truly looks forward to "the talk" - that awkward conversation about the birds and the bees. In many families, it's the father who pulls his son aside for a blunt chat or a few muttered warnings. In my case, there was no father around, so the duty fell to my mom.

I was around thirteen when it happened. I'd started growing taller, my voice cracking, and I guess Mom noticed I was becoming more private and curious about things. One evening, after we watched a movie that had a mild romantic subplot, Mom switched off the TV and looked over at me thoughtfully. I had a sinking feeling something was coming.

"James," she began gently, "you're getting older. We should probably talk about, you know, growing up... and girls... and all that." Her cheeks flushed the tiniest bit, and I realized with a mix of horror and admiration that she was as nervous as I was.

"Mom, please - " I immediately protested, face hot. I could already feel the embarrassment crawling up my neck.

She held up a hand, half-smiling. "I know, I know. It's awkward. But it's important. I want you to hear these things from me, someone who loves you, rather than from rumours or the internet." And so it began. We sat there on the couch, the room dim except for the soft lamp light, and my mother gave me an honest, open talk about sex, respect, and responsibility. She kept her voice calm and matter-of-fact, explaining the basic biology of what happens to boys and girls at our age (which I'd learned in school health class, but still cringed to discuss with *my mom*). I remember staring very hard at a spot on the carpet, wishing I could sink into it.

Sensing my embarrassment, Mom chuckled. "Hey," she said softly, "I know this is uncomfortable. It is for me too. But I don't want it to be a taboo between us. You can always ask me anything. Okay?"

I managed a nod, still avoiding eye contact. She went on to cover the bases: how to stay safe, the importance of consent ("No means no, and yes must be clear," she emphasized), and that it was perfectly normal to have urges and feelings. What struck me most was how she framed everything in terms of respect and care. "Sex isn't just a physical act," she said. "It has emotional consequences too. If you're not ready to handle those, you're not ready for sex. And you must always respect the girl - her feelings, her boundaries, everything."

At one point, she even used an analogy that made it all more annoying: she compared intimacy to driving a car - you shouldn't do it until you're responsible enough to handle the road. I buried my face in my hands, mumbling, "Mooom..." in mortification. She laughed and apologized for the cheesiness, but I have to admit, the point stuck.

As awkward as it was, looking back, I'm profoundly grateful for how she handled it. She didn't threaten me with hellfire or lecture that "boys will be boys." She treated me like a young adult, deserving of truth and capable of making good choices if properly informed. She also made sure to let me know that sexuality was natural and nothing to be ashamed of, as long as it came with responsibility and respect.

After we survived that conversation, I scurried off to my room, eager to escape further embarrassment. But I remember peeking back into the living room and seeing Mom exhale and rub her temples, like she'd just finished a particularly daunting task. It hit me that night how much courage it took for her to fill both parental roles - to talk to her son about things a father might have, and to do it with such grace.

In doing so, she set a tone for honesty between us that carried through the rest of my teen years. I learned that awkward conversations are sometimes the most important ones to have. By addressing something as personal as sex so frankly, she implicitly taught me that I should approach all important discussions - with future partners, friends, or my own children one day - with the same honesty and respect. And yes, I did so well and I am convinced it worked since I am still currently living that life.

# Lesson 7 - Watch Your Tone

Teenagerhood wasn't so exciting for either me or my mom, though, now that I've come to think about it closely. Like many teenagers, I went through a phase where I thought I had everything figured out and God, was I arrogant! It was like I had created some sort of shield against the society and my shield was being rude. During this period, there were several brawls between Mom and I; most of the time, we just moved on and so I don't get to remember it all but I do remember one very night. That night, it had all built up.

By fifteen, I was taller, my voice was deeper, and I had a stubborn streak that flared up more often than I'd like to admit. One evening, that streak collided with my mother's patience in an ugly way.

It was a school night and I was in the living room, sprawled on the couch playing a video game. My backpack lay untouched by the door - homework forgotten. Mom got home late from work that night, looking exhausted. I barely glanced up in greeting. She sighed at the sight of my bag. "James, have you finished your homework yet?" she asked, dropping her purse on the dining table.

"Not yet," I mumbled, eyes glued to the flashing screen. In truth, I had no intention of doing it anytime soon. I was absorbed in my game, and teenage logic told me I could always cram it in later.

Mom walked over and switched on the lamp, brightening the room. "Turn that off now. You know the rule - homework before games." Her voice was firm, but I detected weariness too.

I huffed, annoyed at the interruption. "Just ten more minutes," I muttered, not taking my eyes off the game.

She stepped in front of the TV, blocking my view. "Now," she repeated, leaving no room for debate.

Frustration surged inside me. Without thinking, I blurted out, "Why do you always have to nag me? I'm not a little kid!"

Mom's eyes widened at my sharp tone. "Excuse me?" she said, her voice dangerously quiet.

I knew I'd stepped over a line, but I was riding a wave of teenage rebellion and couldn't stop myself. I stood up, taller than her now, and snapped, "I said I'll do it later! Get off my back!"

For a split second, even I couldn't believe I'd spoken to my mother that way. Believe me, teenagerhood is an agonizing mess. It takes more patience to train a teenager, than you ever will, a child. The silence that followed was deafening. Mom just stared at me, hurt and anger warring in her eyes.

"First of all, lower your voice," she said in a low, controlled tone. "And second, don't you ever speak to me like that again."

Her jaw was set, and I could see the muscles tense in her cheeks. But I was too riled up, full of a teenage sense of invincibility. Instead of apologizing, I doubled down. "You're not a man!" I challenged, my voice dripping with sarcasm. "You can't just boss me around like I'm some soldier or something!"

It was the second time of my life that I reminded Mom that I never had a father - directly or indirectly.

The moment those words left my mouth, I saw something break in her expression. I hadn't fully realized it in my anger. Her face flushed, not just with anger now but with a kind of pain.

Without a word, she walked over to the game console and, with a click, turned it off. The screen went black. I opened my mouth to protest, but she fixed me with a stare that pinned me in place. "Go to your room, James," she said softly. The quiet of her voice was scarier than any shout.

I hesitated, still angry but suddenly unsure. "What - ?"

"Go. To. Your. Room," she repeated, enunciating each word. "Now."

Something in her eyes told me not to push further. I grabbed my backpack and stomped down the hallway to my bedroom, acting all huffy, but inside I was shaken. I slammed my door for good measure, tossing my backpack on the floor. My chest heaved with residual anger, but already I felt a creeping guilt. I'd never spoken to Mom like that before. The look on her face... it made me feel like the worst son in the world.

I flopped onto my bed and stared at the ceiling, adrenaline ebbing and remorse trickling in. Through the thin wall, I could hear the clink of dishes as Mom presumably made herself a late dinner. She didn't call me out or come to my door for a long time. The house was eerily quiet, except for those kitchen sounds and the muffled noise of the TV she eventually turned on in the living room. I imagined her sitting alone, trying not to cry. The thought made my throat tighten.

After what felt like hours (but was probably twenty minutes), I couldn't take it anymore. I got up, opened my door quietly, and peered down the hall. The living room light was off now, and the blue glow of the TV flickered over my mom on the couch. She was just sitting there in the semi-dark, not really watching the show on the screen. She looked lost in thought, or maybe just too tired to move.

I walked over slowly, my socked feet silent on the floor. "Mom?" I said softly.

She turned to look at me. Even in the dim light, I could see her eyes were shiny with unshed tears. Seeing that nearly undid me. I shuffled my feet, not knowing exactly how to begin. "I... I'm sorry," I managed to say.

Her face crumpled for a moment, and she quickly wiped a hand across her eyes. She clicked off the TV, then said, "Come here."

I came closer, my shoulders hunched in shame. She patted the couch next to her, and I sat down. We were quiet for a moment. Finally, in a voice barely above a whisper, she asked, "Do you really think I'm trying to boss you around for no reason? That I'm on your back just to make your life miserable?"

I shook my head vigorously. "No... no, I don't. I was just being stupid."

She sighed. "I know you're growing up. You think I don't understand what it's like to be fifteen and wanting freedom?" She gave a short, sad laugh. "Believe it or not, I was fifteen once too. And I had my share of attitude with my parents."

That was hard to imagine - my mom, who was usually so composed, being a brat like me. But the ghost of a smile on her lips told me she just might have been.

"It's okay to outgrow some things, James," she continued, more firmly now. "But respect is not one of those things. You do not outgrow the expectation to treat people - especially your mother - with basic decency. I know I'm not your father," she added, her voice tightening a bit on the word. "But I am the parent you do have. I deserve the same respect as any father would, if not more, because I'm doing this on my own."

Her words hit me like a series of thumps to the chest. I had no answer. I just stared at my hands. After a moment, I felt her hand cover mine. It was warm, a little callused from a day of work.

"I work hard all day and come home tired," she said softly. "I shouldn't have to come home to fighting with my son. I ask you to do things like homework because I care about you, because I want you to have a good future. Not because I enjoy nagging. You understand?"

I nodded, tears pricking my eyes now.

She put an arm around me and pulled me into a hug. I rested my head on her shoulder, feeling both six years old and strangely grown up at the same time. "I love you," she said into my hair. "But I won't tolerate disrespect. Not from you or anyone. *You're better than that.*"

Believe me, that hit deeper than I had seen coming.

## Lesson 8 - No Shortcuts

If there was one thing my mother refused to tolerate, it was laziness - especially when it came to taking care of our home and responsibilities. Like many other women around the world, she couldn't even bear an ounce of it; something a dad may most likely look over, especially in terms of homely chores. As a preteen, I wasn't exactly a fan of chores or routines like I was in my childhood stages. Other concepts were already kicking in - like ways to actually start earning money. I'd try every trick in the book to finish my tasks faster so I could get back to doing what I liked or let me say - what I considered important. But Mom had a saying she'd drilled into me: "If you're going to do something, do it right." That lesson in self-discipline came into sharp focus one particular Saturday morning.

In our house, Saturdays began early. While other kids slept in or watched cartoons, Mom would be waking me up at dawn with a gentle nudge and a cheerful, "Rise and shine, it's chore time!" I'd groan and bury myself deeper under the covers, but there was no escape. By 7 a.m., I was usually dressed and grumpily munching cereal, eyed by my mother who was already organizing the cleaning supplies.

On this Saturday, my main job was to clean the bathroom and mop the kitchen floor while Mom tackled laundry and yard work. I was 12 and had recently developed an attitude that I was too old to be told how to do such "simple" things. So, when Mom reminded me, "Don't forget to scrub behind the toilet and rinse out the mop when you're done," I just rolled my eyes and muttered, "Yeah, yeah, I know."

I shut the bathroom door and got to work - sort of. Five minutes in, I grew impatient with scrubbing the tub. The soap scum was stubborn and my arm was getting tired. Surely "good enough" would suffice? I swiped the sponge half-heartedly over the remaining spots, decided that looked okay, and moved on. For the floor, instead of properly sweeping up the corners, I hurriedly ran the mop across the tiles, figuring the soapy water would push any dirt out of sight.

In record time, I emerged, announcing that I was finished. Mom was in the kitchen, sorting laundry into the machine. She looked surprised. "Already? That was fast."

"Yup, all done," I declared, trying to sound convincing.

She narrowed her eyes slightly. "Alright. Let's have a look."

I felt a pang of dread as she stepped past me into the bathroom. I trailed after her, heart thumping. The bathroom looked clean at first glance - it certainly smelled of lemon cleanser. Maybe she wouldn't notice the details.

Mom's silence as she inspected the sink and tub was telling. Then she crouched to peer behind the base of the toilet. A small dust bunny, which I'd neglected to sweep, clung to the baseboard. She didn't say anything - she didn't need to. The disapproval was clear on her face as she stood up.

"James," she said, turning to me with a frown, "does this look *done right* to you?"

I flushed with embarrassment. "I... I guess I missed a spot."

Mom crossed her arms. "More than a spot. It seems you decided to rush through instead of doing it properly."

Caught red-handed, I bristled defensively. "It's just a bathroom, Mom. It's going to get dirty again anyway! Why spend so much time on it?"

She took a deep breath, the kind that means she's gathering patience. "Come here," she said, motioning me into the small bathroom with her. I stepped in, feeling sulky. She pointed at the tub. "Would you want to take a bath with that grime still there?" she asked.

I looked at the faint filmy streaks I'd left. "No..." I admitted quietly.

She handed me the sponge I'd tossed aside. "Then do it again. And this time, actually put some elbow grease into it. No shortcuts."

I knew from her tone that arguing was pointless. So I went at the tub again, this time scrubbing each inch until it gleamed. Mom stood by the door, supervising in silence. My pride smarted - I felt like a little kid being watched - but I also felt a grudging determination to prove I could do it right.

After I re-mopped the floor (picking up that dust bunny and the dirt I'd shoved into a corner), the bathroom truly was spotless. My arms were sore, and it had taken twice as long as my sloppy attempt. But when Mom inspected now, she nodded in approval. "Much better. See the difference?"

I had to admit I did. The tiles shone, the tub was pure white, and even the air felt fresher. Oddly, instead of feeling annoyed, I felt a small swell of pride and so subtly, I figured that self-discipline means doing what needs to be done, the right way, even when you'd rather be doing anything else.

Over time, those Saturday mornings paid off. I found that the satisfaction of a job well done - even something as small as a clean bathroom - felt better than the hollow "victory" of finishing fast with half-hearted effort. My mother taught me to take pride in doing things properly. There are no real shortcuts in life without cost, a truth I carry with me in everything from work projects to personal goals.

## Lesson 9 - The Bigger Person

In middle school I had my first run-in with a school bully. Many of us had this experience as kids, and what our parents did when such news came to them shaped our perception afterwards greatly. I was eleven, skinny and bookish, an easy target for a tougher kid looking to throw his weight around. One afternoon during recess, this boy - Damon was his name - decided it would be fun to shove me off the tetherball court and call me some names. I still recall the sting of gravel in my palms as I caught myself from falling, and the hot flush of anger and embarrassment that rushed to my face as other kids watched.

"Do something about it!" one of my friends hissed after Damon swaggered off, having stolen our ball but nope, I stood there trembling with fury and humiliation. Part of me wanted to run after Damon and tackle him, or at least shout a clever insult back. But I was scared, too - he was bigger and had a reputation for fighting.

That day I walked home stewing in silence. Mom immediately sensed something was wrong when I slumped in, late and dirty. She raised an eyebrow at my scuffed elbows and torn shirt. "You get into a fight, James?" she asked quietly.

I shook my head. "Not... exactly. This kid at school pushed me. Took our ball. I didn't fight him, but... I wanted to." My voice quavered with a mix of shame and anger. Yes, I remember every feeling and mood that came with that experience. You don't easily forget this, trust me.

Mom set down the groceries she had been unpacking and gestured for me to sit at the kitchen table. I plopped down, and she sat across from me, concern etched on her face. Gently, she asked me to tell her what happened. The story tumbled out - how Damon had bullied me and how worthless it made me feel in front of everyone.

After I finished, I waited for Mom to either get upset on my behalf or maybe tell me I should have defended myself. She did neither immediately. She reached over and took my hand (which still had a couple pieces of grit from the playground embedded in the skin). "I'm sorry that happened to you," she said softly.

"That boy was wrong to treat you that way."

I nodded, feeling a lump in my throat. "I was so mad, Mom. I wanted to punch him," I confessed.

She squeezed my hand. "I know that feeling. But listen... Getting into a fistfight can lead to even bigger problems. You could get hurt badly, or in trouble at school. There are other ways to handle this."

I frowned. "Like what? Just let him bully me?"

Her eyes flashed a little with resolve. "No. Being peaceful doesn't mean being a doormat. You can stand up for yourself without throwing punches."

That was when she said the words: "Be the bigger person." I couldn't get what she meant by that immediately so she went further to give details and ensure the message was well passed.

The next time Damon tried something, I should look him in the eye, speak in a steady voice, and tell him to stop - loud enough for others to hear. Bullies, she explained, often back down when they see you won't cower. And if that didn't work, I was to walk away and inform a teacher rather than escalate it myself. I remember scrunching up my face at the "tell a teacher" part, worried that might label me a snitch. But Mom added:

*"There's no shame in getting help when someone is hurting you. You have a right to feel safe."*

"Dad would've just told me to hit him back," I mumbled, voicing a thought that had popped into my head. I had no actual dad to say that, but I'd heard the advice from TV shows and some friends' fathers. *Stand your ground.* Fight back.

Mom pursed her lips. "Maybe. I'm not your dad, but I am telling you this: real strength sometimes means using your head and heart, not your fists."

Damon did try to bully me again. As it is, once the bullies get you once, you become a regular prey. This time, he cornered me by the bike racks after school, flicking the back of my head and calling me names in front of his buddies. My stomach was doing flips of fear. It didn't mean I didn't try though. I took a deep breath, stood up straight, and in a loud, clear voice I said, "Leave me alone, Damon." It wasn't entirely true - I was quaking inside - but I forced myself to hold his gaze. It worked, at least for that day. He backed off with a shrug, muttering that I "wasn't worth it."

I went home extremely eager to tell Mom what happened. She was more than proud of me. It didn't work all the time though and it was just a matter of time before I figured it was something that built up within you and with the continuous actions of standing up for yourself without the exertion of violence, you eventually became "the bigger person."

## Lessons Live Forever

Looking back on these lessons, I'm overwhelmed with gratitude. Mom imparted wisdom in moments big and small, equipping me with a moral compass, a compassionate heart, and resilience in adversity. Yet, I also recognize what was missing. As I grew into adolescence, I became more acutely aware that I had learned almost everything about being a good person from a woman - but I still yearned to understand what it meant to be a man.

That journey to seek out explicitly masculine lessons - through mentors, uncles, and public figures - is its own story, one that unfolded as I left boyhood behind.

# CHAPTER 3

# MASCULINITY WITHOUT A MANUAL

By the time I entered my early teens, I'd begun to realize just how many voices were telling me what a "real man" should be; and how none of those voices sounded like my mother's. Up until then, everything I knew about strength, courage, and kindness came from watching Mom. She had taught me how to ride a bike, how to say "please" and "thank you," how to stand up for myself without knocking anyone else down. But as I moved through adolescence, I felt more and more like I was missing some secret guidebook; a manual handed down from father to son; on how to be a man. Every direction I turned, a different map was being thrust at me. At school, the loudest boys bragged about how tough they were, how many punches they could take and laughs they could fake. On TV and in music, the men who looked like me; the ones held up as examples; swaggered with confidence, muscles bulging and voices booming, never a tear in their eye unless it was rage. Even among friends, there were unspoken rules: talk this way, walk that way, don't be... "soft."

I was overwhelmed.

I tried my best to navigate this maze of mixed signals. It felt like stepping into a new world without a compass. One moment, a teacher praised me for being thoughtful and gentle with a classmate who was crying; the next moment, a kid in the hallway snickered and called me a mama's boy because I helped pick up a girl's dropped books. In one breath I'd hear *"speak up, be assertive"* and in the next *"real men don't talk about their feelings."* The contradictions were everywhere, and I was smack in the middle of them, trying to piece together an identity out of fragments.

## The Man Act

I remember one afternoon when I was about thirteen, standing in front of the bathroom mirror, alone in the house, practicing how to lower my voice; yes, as crazy as it may seem. Puberty had just started sprinkling some fuzz above my lip and stretching me taller. I'd lock the door, stare at my reflection, and try on different faces; stern, unbothered, cool. Deepening my voice from its natural tenor to what I imagined was a more manly register, I'd say tough-guy lines I picked up from movies: "Don't mess with me," "Yeah, whatever." I even practiced a stony, unflinching stare, the kind I saw my favourite action movie hero give right before he saved the day. But inevitably, I'd catch my own eye in the mirror and burst out laughing at how silly I looked. There I was, a skinny kid with toothpaste smudges on the sink, trying to playact some Hollywood idea of a man. My laugh would crack the facade; literally cracking back into my not-yet-deep voice. In those mirror moments, relief and embarrassment mingled; I was glad no one was watching, but I also felt foolish for even trying. *Why did this feel so hard?*

Still, that urge to try on manhood in different ways only grew stronger. In the absence of a father at home, I looked to the world around me for templates. I devoured comic books and noted how the heroes always stood tall, fists on hips, unafraid of anything. I listened to rap albums where men boasted about never backing down and having hearts made of steel. On weekends, I'd plant myself in front of the TV to watch basketball games, absorbing how the star players would pound their chests after a good play or snarl in the face of trash-talk from the other team. I took mental notes everywhere: how the older boys in the neighbourhood walked with a bit of a limp in their stride (a swagger I secretly practiced), how they greeted each other with elaborate handshakes and playful jabs like *"What's up, man?"* or sometimes rougher insults that somehow counted as friendship. It was like studying for an exam with no teacher to guide me and an endless curriculum of contradictory lessons.

One week, being a man seemed to mean being tough above all; so I tried that on. I started wearing a frown like some sort of armor, keeping my face set in what I hoped looked like bored confidence. When guys horsed around in the hallways, shoving each other into lockers, I'd join in with a bit of extra force. Not enough to really hurt anyone; I wasn't built for that, frankly; but enough that I wouldn't be seen as weak. I even attempted to pepper my speech with bravado. If someone asked how I was doing, instead of my usual "I'm good," I'd throw in something cocky like, "I'm chillin', always chillin'," with a slow nod I'd copied from a music video. Inside, I cringed each time I tried these affectations, half expecting someone to burst out laughing at my act. Sometimes they did: a close friend might snort and say, "What're you so serious about?" or mimic my forced deep voice. But other times, I noticed a difference; a couple of the rowdier kids gave me approving nods, as if I'd spoken some secret password. It was intoxicating in a way, that tiny dose of male approval. I found myself pushing a bit further, testing how far I could go in this performance.

I even tried changing my look to match the image of "cool" I saw around me. I begged Mom for a pair of name-brand sneakers that all the popular guys were wearing. When I finally got them (after saving up and some pleading), I strutted into school thinking I'd feel transformed. They were nice shoes, sure, but they didn't magically make me more confident. Another time I borrowed a baggy jacket and a fake gold chain from a friend for the weekend, trying to emulate the swagger of a rapper I admired. Mom raised an amused eyebrow when I walked in with pants sagging and cap turned backward. "Is this my son or a music video extra?" she teased. Embarrassed, I burst out laughing; I looked ridiculous and we both knew it. So much for costumes making the man.

## A Channel for Anger

That's how I ended up at the edge of Ridley Park one sweltering day after school, with a knot of eighth-grade boys who all had something to prove. Ridley Park was a scrappy patch of grass and dirt behind our middle school where, when the teachers weren't watching, the kids settled their differences with their fists. I'd never been in a real fight before. I was the kid who solved math problems and drew comic strips, not the one who threw punches during recess. But that day, I strayed from my usual route home and followed the others, heart pounding in my throat. Part of me was terrified; I knew fights were stupid and I didn't really want to hurt anyone or get hurt. But another part of me was fuelled by a cocktail of curiosity and adrenaline. *What kind of man would I be if I ran away from a challenge? Didn't every boy have to get into a fight at least once to earn his stripes?*

The "challenge" in question was a scuffle between one of my friends, Rico, and a stocky boy named DeShawn over something trivial; a shove on the basketball court that afternoon, some trash talk that went too far. It didn't matter; by the time we were all huddled in the park's dusty clearing, the details were lost to the chants of *"Fight! Fight!"* around us. I hung back at first, just another face in the circle of spectators as Rico and DeShawn squared off, but then I heard one of DeShawn's buddies snicker, *"Rico's crew got no dads at home; no wonder they don't know how to act."* The words sliced through the air and, before I knew it, through me. My vision tunnelled for a second as hot anger flared in my chest. He might as well have thrown a match on gasoline. All the embarrassment, the quiet hurt of being the boy without a dad, ignited into something fierce and reckless.

Without thinking, I stepped forward and shot back, "Say that again?" My voice came out low and harsh, an almost unfamiliar growl. Part of me couldn't believe I was inserting myself into this; I wasn't even the one being challenged! But some instinct, or maybe pride, propelled me. DeShawn's friend; a tall kid named Marcus; sneered and looked me up and down. "You heard me," he said. "No daddy at home to teach y'all how to fight." He barely got the last word out before, to my own shock, I lunged at him.

What happened next was a blur of flailing limbs and raw, unpractised aggression. Marcus was older and heavier; he had a bit of a moustache already and clearly some experience brawling. I, on the other hand, had only my adrenaline and pent-up frustration. We collided with an awkward thud and tumbled to the ground, kicking up a cloud of dust. I swung wildly, landing a hit on his shoulder, which might as well have been a feather landing on a rock. He responded with a fist that glanced off my cheek and sent a lightning bolt of pain through my face. No, it wasn't funny. The circle of kids exploded with noise; some cheering, some jeering. I heard Rico yell my name in alarm or encouragement; I couldn't tell. For a few chaotic seconds, all I knew was the tangle of fists and knees, the taste of copper in my mouth where I'd bitten my cheek, and a red haze of anger that kept me throwing punches even as my mind screamed *What are you doing?!*

The fight was over almost as soon as it started. Marcus managed to pin me down, my back scratching against the dirt and dried grass. I stared up at the sky, breathing hard, arms pinned under his knees. I braced for a punch that never came. Instead, he just gave me a shove of disgust and got off me, spitting to the side. "Not so mouthy now, huh?" he muttered. Someone; probably one of Rico's friends; helped me up. My head was ringing and I realized I'd lost a shoe in the skirmish; one socked foot stood in the dust until a girl from my class shyly handed me my sneaker with an awkward half-smile. What I remember most, though, is the silence that followed. The crowd was already dispersing, the show over. My cheek throbbed and when I gingerly touched it, my fingertips came away bloody from my split lip. But worse than the physical pain was the sick feeling swirling in my stomach. I had stepped into this fight trying to defend my pride, to prove something; but all I felt now was humiliation.

As I limped away from Ridley Park with Rico, I tried to play it off. "He got lucky," I mumbled through my swollen lip. Rico, nursing a bruise on his temple from his own scrap with DeShawn, just shook his head. "Man, why'd you jump in like that?" he asked, not unkindly. I didn't have a good answer. How could I explain that Marcus's comment had hit the bullseye of an insecurity I barely admitted having? How could I say that in that moment I wasn't really thinking about him or the fight at all; I was thinking about my father, or the lack of one, and how badly I wanted to erase the target that absence seemed to paint on me? So I just shrugged. "He was talking trash," I muttered. "Had to shut him up." Rico was quiet for a minute, then clapped a hand on my shoulder. "Still," he offered, "that was... kind of brave, I guess." He tried to catch my eye and I could tell he meant it. It was a thank you, and I managed a nod. But inside, I didn't feel brave.

I felt stupid.

When I got home that evening, my mother took one look at my face and gasped. I had carefully planned my arrival; slipping in through the back door, hoping to head straight to my room; but Mom was waiting in the kitchen, as she often was, a half-chopped onion on the cutting board in front of her. The smell of sautéing garlic hung in the air. She turned, wiping her hands on a dish towel, and her expression went from tired to alarmed in an instant. "Oh my goodness, what happened?" She rushed over, the dish towel now dabbing at my cheek and chin before I could even open my mouth to answer.

"I'm fine," I tried to say, but it came out garbled with her fussing. She held my chin, tilting my face to inspect the damage. Her eyes flared with that mix of anger and worry I knew so well; the same look she had when I'd come home late the time I snuck out, the same look as when I broke my arm falling off the jungle gym in third grade. It was the *you could-have-been-hurt terror that always ended up as you're-in-trouble-now* determination.

"Who did this to you?" she demanded, voice taut. I winced, not just from the sting of peroxide she'd begun swiping on my cut lip, but from the question itself. If I told her the truth; that I had jumped into a fight on purpose; I knew exactly how she'd react. And it wouldn't be pride in my macho display. It would be disappointment, maybe even hurt. She'd wonder if she was losing her sweet boy to something ugly.

"It was an accident," I lied quickly. Mom paused, narrowing her eyes. I wasn't usually a good liar, but I tried to sell it. "Some of us were just goofing around, and I, uh, tripped and ate dirt. It's nothing." I forced a grin, which I'm sure looked pitiful with my swollen lip.

Mom's lips pressed into a thin line as she continued cleaning me up. A cotton ball dabbed with rubbing alcohol hovered over a scrape on my chin, making me flinch. "This doesn't look like nothing," she said quietly. I avoided her gaze. Her hands were gentle but I could feel the question hanging between us. She knew I wasn't telling the whole truth; I sensed her trying to decide whether to push.

After a long pause, she sighed. "Alright. Go wash up properly and change out of those dirty clothes," she said, voice softening a bit. "Dinner will be ready soon." That was it. She let it drop, at least for now. As I slunk to the bathroom, I felt a wave of relief; and guilt. Mom always knew when I was hurting, but she also knew when to give me space to come to her on my own. I think she recognized that this was one of those times.

Later that night, I lay in bed staring at the ceiling, replaying the fight and its aftermath on a loop. In the next room, I heard Mom's low voice on the phone, probably talking to Aunt Nia; a fellow nurse that worked at the clinic; or one of her friends, as she often did late in the evening. I caught snippets: "*...he's okay, just a scrape... boys... wish his father...*" and then her voice dropped too low for me to make out the rest. I closed my eyes against a hot prickling of tears. I hated the thought of her worrying about me like that, maybe even feeling guilty that she couldn't prevent something or that she couldn't give me whatever a father might have.

These were late-night thoughts I never voiced aloud. What I did know was that earlier, when I was scrambling on the ground with Marcus, all I could think was, *Is this what being a man is? Is this what I'm supposed to do?* Because if it was, it felt awful.

Lying there in the dark, I gently touched the tender spot on my cheek and felt a swell of conflicting emotions. I was angry at Marcus for what he said, angry at my father for not being there; because if he were, maybe kids like Marcus wouldn't see me as an easy target. But I was also angry at myself. I let someone's words push me into being someone I wasn't.

The truth was, I didn't like fighting. I didn't get any thrill from the brief flash of violence.

*I had stepped up to defend my pride, but in doing*
*so I'd stepped out of who I really was.*

I rolled onto my side and the bedsprings creaked softly. On my desk, comic books were stacked in a messy pile. A basketball jersey hung off the back of my chair. Art and sports; two things I genuinely liked. Not for proving anything, just for me. I realized in that moment that I felt most like myself when I was absorbed in drawing a new comic hero or shooting hoops alone at the playground, not when I was trying to imitate what I thought others expected. *So why was I so desperate to wear these different masks of manhood that didn't fit?*

I thought about something Mom often told me, a gentle refrain whenever I came to her insecure about something: "*Who you are is already enough.*" She said it the first time I got teased in elementary school for bringing homemade lunch instead of store-bought snacks, and again the time I worried I wasn't "cool" because I still secretly liked cartoons at age twelve. Each time, she'd hug me and remind me that being myself was more important than being what others wanted me to be. Already enough, I mouthed to myself in the dark. It was a comforting thought, but one I struggled to fully believe now that I was in the thick of teen-age chaos.

I wish I could say that night ended with a tidy revelation, that I swore off caring about macho posturing from then on. Life is rarely that neat. But it was the first time I truly confronted the growing divide inside me. There was the person I wanted to be; *compassionate, creative, maybe a little quiet*; and the person I felt I had to perform; *tough, unaffected, always in control.* And I understood, with a clarity that made my chest ache, that if I kept chasing those stereotypes, I might lose the real me completely.

The next day at school, I walked through the halls still sporting a faint bruise on my face. Marcus and his crew barely gave me a glance, the issue apparently settled. If anything, I got a few nods of respect from some classmates, like Hey, you stood up for yourself. But I wasn't proud. I didn't feel like I'd proven myself; only that I'd betrayed myself a little.

# The Thompson Encounter

A few afternoons later, I found myself in the school library avoiding the heat, thumbing through a dusty anthology of poems. I'd taken to slipping into the library after classes; a sanctuary of sorts from the noise outside. Hardly any kids our age hung out there on purpose, which made it perfect. I could sink into a corner armchair without any eyes on me and decompress. On this particular day I was flipping mindlessly, not really reading, when our English teacher, Mr. Thompson, came by pushing a cart of books. He was one of those teachers who everyone liked; mid-thirties, enthusiastic, known for sneaking philosophical questions into literature class and making even the slackers think for a minute. He also ran an after-school creative writing club that I was secretly considering joining, though I hadn't worked up the nerve.

"Taking up poetry, are we?" he said as he noticed what I was holding. I straightened up, feeling caught. "Oh, uh, just killing time," I mumbled, somewhat embarrassed to be seen with a poetry book. That didn't exactly jibe with the tough image I'd been dabbling in. But Mr. Thompson only smiled. He nodded at the seat across from me. "Mind if I join you for a minute?"

I shook my head, and he sat down, resting his arms on the cart handle. Then he nodded toward my slowly healing bruise. "Heard you got into a bit of a scrape last week," he said gently. I tensed up, looking down. "Don't worry," he added quickly, "I'm not here to lecture you. I just wanted to check in."

I swallowed, still not meeting his gaze. "I'm fine," I said quietly. Mr. Thompson was silent, and finally I looked up. His eyes were kind, patient.

"You know," he said thoughtfully, "when I was your age, I got into a few fights myself." That surprised me. Mr. Thompson was bookish and calm, not someone I pictured exchanging blows. "Yeah," he continued, as if reading my mind, "I thought it was what I had to do to prove I wasn't a pushover. Most times, it started over someone insulting me or a friend. And I always regretted it afterwards."

I felt a lump in my throat. He wasn't saying it explicitly, but I sensed an understanding there; maybe even that he knew why I fought. I wondered how much he knew about me. I wasn't sure what to say, so I just nodded faintly.

He leaned back a bit. "It's tricky, isn't it? Growing up, figuring out how you're supposed to act. Especially when everyone's telling you different things." I glanced at him, unsure if this was a trap. It didn't feel like it. It felt like he actually cared. "I guess," I said.

Mr. Thompson gave a small smile. "I won't pry. Just remember, it's okay to make your own definition of what being a man means. There's no one right way, no matter what some people say." He nodded at the poetry book in my hand. "If you like poetry, read poetry. If you feel like fighting... well, try writing about it instead."

I couldn't help but let out a tiny laugh through my nose. It sounded almost ridiculous; write about a fight? But part of me was intrigued by that idea. I realized I still had so much adrenaline and emotion swirling from that incident, and nowhere to put it. Perhaps scribbling it down could help. You'll be surprised at the extent to which little advices from people around you could lead you in life.

Mr. Thompson stood, patting the cart. "There's a great poem in that collection about courage. Page 72. Check it out sometime." He began to roll away, then paused. "And if you ever want to drop by the writing club, we'd love to have you. No pressure."

I watched him leave, a strange mix of relief and longing settling in my chest. Relief that he hadn't scolded me or pressed too hard. Longing because I wished, not for the first time, that I had a man like that in my family; someone who just got it, someone who could offer a roadmap or at least a sounding board. In a small way, Mr. Thompson's words were like a hand on my shoulder, steadying me. I flipped to page 72 and found the poem, then quickly checked the book out to take home.

## The Powerful Art of Writing It Down

That evening, after finishing my homework, I did something I'd never done before. I pulled out an old notebook and, under the soft glow of my bedside lamp, I tried to write about the fight. I wasn't writing this as some tough guy recounting my victory, there was no victory to speak of, but about how it felt.

I wrote about the anger that flared when Marcus insulted me, how it felt like something provoked not just by him but by all the times someone had pitied me or prodded at that father-shaped gap in my life. I wrote about the shame that came right after the fight, and the confusion of what I thought being a man meant in that moment. I scribbled until my handwriting turned sloppy and my hand ached. I can say for a fact that it wasn't a poem or anything worthy of the school literary magazine, but it was honest. In a weird way, it felt like I was talking to myself; the real me, not the one I pretended to be with others. By the end, a few teardrops had smudged the ink.

*Writing provides more clarity than you can ever imagine.*

I never showed anyone that notebook, but I kept it. It became a kind of safety valve in the months that followed; my private space to say the things I didn't think I could say out loud. On the outside, I might still try on the occasional mask: laughing along at jokes I didn't find funny, or flexing in the mirror wondering if more muscle would automatically grant me respect. But I was getting closer, little by little, to understanding that those masks suffocated me more than they protected me. And writing became an anchor for me to keep pushing. I still write till this very day - hell, I wrote this book, didn't I?

## Strength and Tenderness

One evening, a few months later, Mom and I were watching a movie in our living room. It was an old comedy she loved, something from decades ago with slapstick scenes. We were piled on our thrift-store couch under a knitted blanket. I chuckled at the actors' antics, but my mind was partly elsewhere, turning over the puzzle of masculinity that I seemed to face daily. The fight in the park had blown over, but new situations had popped up to take its place: the older boys at school boasting about girls they'd "conquered" while I sat mute, too inexperienced and frankly uninterested in treating relationships like trophies - the moment I hesitated during a pickup basketball game because I saw a kid twist his ankle, and I went to help him up instead of charging down the court - earning me a *"Man, you're soft"* from a teammate. Each incident on its own was small, but together they formed a pattern I was becoming keenly aware of.

I must have been frowning because Mom nudged me. "Penny for your thoughts?" she said softly. On the screen, the movie characters were in the middle of a pie fight, cream and crust flying humorously. I didn't want to burden her with my adolescent identity crisis; she had enough to worry about; but she looked at me with that gentle invitation and suddenly I found myself speaking.

"Mom," I began, keeping my eyes on the TV, "did you ever worry if I'd, you know, learn how to be a man? Without... well, you know." I trailed off, unsure how to reference my father. We rarely talked about him unless I asked directly.

Mom muted the television, the sudden quiet making my heart thump. I glanced over; she was studying me, trying to read where the question was coming from. She didn't look upset, just thoughtful. "I did worry," she admitted, tucking a leg under her on the couch to face me better. "Not because I didn't think I could raise you, but because I know there are some things I can't teach from experience; like how it feels to be a man in this world."

Her honesty was like a balm and a new sting at once. "So how did you... I mean, why didn't you ever try to, I dunno, find me a male role model or something?" I didn't mean it accusatorially; I was genuinely curious. Some of my friends had Big Brothers from programs, or uncles who took them to ballgames. For us, it had always just been us.

Mom sighed softly, a small smile on her face. "I thought about it. But I guess I believed that if I filled our home with enough love and good values, you'd find the pieces you needed, even if you had to look outside our walls sometimes." She reached over and smoothed my hair; a gesture that normally might make me squirm at my age, but tonight I let her. "And I hoped that the men who did cross your path; teachers, coaches; would show you by example how to be good and kind and strong. Not just strong in muscles, but in here." She tapped my chest, over my heart.

I felt a warmth in my chest at her words, but I also felt a wave of sadness. "It's just hard sometimes," I admitted, my voice barely above a whisper. "Everyone's saying different things about what I should be. Sometimes I feel like I'm doing it all wrong." My face burned saying it aloud; I realized I was confessing a kind of failure, or at least that's how it felt to me.

Mom's eyes glistened. She took my hand. "Listen to me," she said gently but firmly. *"There is no single way to be a man.* Anyone who tells you there is, is lying or has a very small imagination. Being a man, being a woman, being a person... it comes down to the kind of heart you have and the actions you take. You are not doing it wrong. You are growing, learning, *and that's never a straight line."*

I looked at her; this woman who had taught me nearly everything I knew about being a human; and I realized how much of what was good in me came from her. My throat tightened. "I just... maybe I feel like I have to prove I'm not missing anything. To other people. To myself," I added the last part quietly.

Her face softened even more, and she squeezed my hand. "I know, baby. I know. People will always have their opinions, their 'single stories' about what your life must be. But you don't have to prove anything to anyone. *You just keep being you, and the kind of man you are will shine through."*

*Strength and tenderness* are not opposites. I can be both. I can learn from everyone around me, but I'll make my own blueprint. Writing it down made it feel real, like an oath. I didn't know it then, but that realization was a turning point. It was a seed of confidence planted in my confused teen heart. It wouldn't sprout fully for years, but it was there, ready.

## None Is Perfect

In the months that followed, I still had my ups and downs. I still mimicked my basketball heroes on the court, trying to talk a little trash (mostly to laugh it off later). I still felt a flush of shame whenever someone made a crack about not having a dad. But I also started to notice something: the men I quietly admired, the ones who seemed comfortable in their own skin, weren't the loudest or the toughest. They were the ones who treated others with respect and carried themselves with a calm assurance.

Like Mr. Thompson, who never raised his voice in class but could silence us with a stern look when we got too rowdy; and who also spent extra time after school helping a struggling student because he cared. Or the neighbour, Mr. Jenkins and his constant support. He once caught me in the hallway as I rushed, frustrated, after failing my first try at the driver's permit test. I must have looked upset because he called me over and shared a story of crashing his father's truck as a teen; told with humour and a "we all mess up, just try again" wink. That small kindness, the way he was unafraid to talk about his own youthful failure, struck me as quietly courageous.

I stored these observations like pieces of a mosaic. None of these men were perfect or had all the answers, but each showed me a glimmer of what manhood could include: patience, empathy, humility, resilience. And none of those qualities required a swagger or a smirk.

One day in the locker room after gym class, a couple of guys were mocking another boy, I looked at her; Alan, for always writing in a journal. I had noticed Alan often scribbling in a notebook before class; he was shy, wore glasses, not really part of any clique. The teasing got a bit harsh; they were calling him "Shakespeare" and "princess" and laughing. Usually, I kept my head down to avoid attention in those moments, but for some reason, as naturally as it could be, I spoke up. "Cut it out, guys," I said, trying to sound casual. "He's not bothering anyone."

The locker room fell silent in that charged way it does when someone breaks the unwritten rule of not intervening. Two of the tormentors looked at me in surprise, not sure if I was serious. Alan stood frozen by his locker, face flushed. I felt a bead of sweat from the postclass shower trickle down my neck, but I kept my expression even. One of the boys, Travis, scoffed, "We're just joking around, man. Why you defending him? You his bodyguard now or something?" There was a challenge in his tone.

I took a breath. "Nah," I said, "I just think it's cool he writes. I mean, who knows, he could be famous one day and we'll all look stupid for not getting an autograph when we had the chance." I flashed a quick grin. A couple of the guys chuckled; the tension broke just a little. Travis rolled his eyes, muttering under his breath as he went back to tying his shoes. But he had gotten bored and let it drop.

As the group moved on to talking about the upcoming basketball game, I caught a glimpse of Alan. He gave me the tiniest nod, gratitude shining in his eyes. Now, that was a moment where I felt more "like a man" than I ever did throwing a punch. I had stood up not for pride or image, but for what felt right. And it felt good.

Walking home that day, gym bag slung over my shoulder, I had a spring in my step. It struck me that building my own blueprint for manhood didn't require constructing something from scratch, but more about assembling pieces I already had: *Mom's compassion, my own creative soul, a dash of courage to speak up when it counted, the humility to accept guidance from wherever it came.* Maybe I didn't have a manual, but I had the materials to write one for myself.

That evening, I scribbled again in my notebook: a rough list of qualities I valued in the men I admired; *kindness, humour, strength (both physical and mental), respect for others, honesty, and being supportive.* Then I circled two that I decided mattered most to me: strength and tenderness. Next to them I wrote: "not opposites."

I was far from having everything figured out; I was still a kid, after all; but as I closed out my early teens, I did so with a growing sense of clarity. I could lift weights and build muscle if I wanted, but it wouldn't make me any more of a man if my character was weak.

I could learn to defend myself, but I didn't have to lose my gentleness to do it. I could admire star athletes or rappers or action heroes, but I didn't have to mimic every part of them; I could pick the bravery or confidence I liked and leave the showboating behind.

In a way, it felt liberating to realize I didn't have to follow someone else's script. It was also a bit scary; there was no template, no father's footsteps to follow, just a path I had to clear on my own. But I wasn't really alone. Mom's early lessons and unwavering love were the foundation beneath me. In her own way, she had been modelling a balance of strength and gentleness all along - playing every role, showing me how caring and firmness could coexist. That was precisely the balance I hoped to carry into my own adult life. And around me, I was beginning to see the world not as a single judgey audience waiting for me to fail, but as a collection of individuals each figuring out their own stuff too. Some of those individuals were handing me nuggets of wisdom without even knowing it.

One weekend, Mom and I volunteered at a community center event, a sort of fair and fundraiser. There was a makeshift stage where local kids performed dances and songs. Backstage, I was helping to set up chairs when I saw a little boy, probably six or seven, crying quietly behind a curtain. I recognized him; he was the son of one of the women organizing the event. She was busy at the mic introducing the next act. I crouched down. "Hey buddy, you okay?" I asked softly. He sniffled and mumbled something about being scared to go on stage for the group sing-along. The easy thing to do; the typical "guy" thing, maybe; would have been to give him a quick "Man up, you got this" pat and carry on. Instead, without really thinking, I sat on the floor next to him. I told him how when I was little, I used to get stage fright too (true story; I'd puked in a trash can before a spelling bee in third grade). I made a goofy face, which earned a tiny giggle. We practiced a couple of the song lines together quietly until his breathing calmed. Eventually, he mustered a shaky smile. "Thanks," he whispered before running off.

It was such a small moment. But I realized as I watched him go that the younger me might have been too self-conscious to do that; to sit on a floor and comfort a scared kid, to let tenderness trump looking cool. I had grown. Not in some dramatic way that others would necessarily notice; I wasn't some paragon of wisdom or anything. But inside, I knew I had begun to choose the kind of man I wanted to be. A man who could be strong when needed, gentle when needed, and true to himself always.

## There May Be a Manual Afterall

Masculinity without a manual: that's what I was living. I realized that my character wasn't built from following a script, but from integrating all the parts of me - the hard and the soft, the bold and the scared. My manual was unconventional, compiled from my mother's love, a patchwork of role models, and a willingness to be both brave and vulnerable. I knew I still had a long journey ahead, and the ache of my father's absence might never disappear entirely. But I was no longer chasing other men's shadows; I had built my own blueprint.

It was a promise to embrace wholeness over hardness, and I felt ready to carry that into whatever came next.

# The Journey

**"It is good to have an end to journey toward; but it is the journey that matters in the end."**
*- Rumi*

# CHAPTER 4

# SCHOOLYARD REALITIES

High school arrived like a tidal wave, sweeping me into a bustling sea of new faces, new challenges, and the same old question: Where do I fit in? At fourteen and fifteen, I found that the stakes felt higher. Reputations formed fast under those harsh fluorescent lights of the school environment. Everyone seemed to have a place. In the cafeteria for instance, the football players crowded one table, the student council kids another, the gamers and anime enthusiasts tucked in a corner; each group staking out territory.

And among the many cliques, I wasn't sure where I belonged.

I floated from table to table some days, or ate with my two close friends outside on the steps, watching the currents of school life flow around us. The social pecking order was clearer than ever, and I felt the pressure to find my footing.

My reality as 'the boy without a dad' occasionally cast a shadow, even when I wished it wouldn't. During the first week of freshman year, when I handed in the contact card with 'Father's Name' blank, the teacher's small, pitying smile felt like an insult. I didn't want hushed compassion; I just wanted to be treated like everyone else; I was too old for that sting.

But in reality, there's no getting over it all of a sudden.

## One-On-One Encounters

The urge to set everything right often led to you making some quite unconventional, risky moves. This happened especially when you encountered a training method different from what you've been used to and see the need to question it. There was one afternoon in gym class when I saw our coach, Mr. Simmons, barking at a smaller kid for missing a layup. The boy's face was red and I could see he was on the verge of tears as Mr. Simmons shouted, "Come on, you gotta toughen up! My grandma can run faster than that!" A few of the more athletic kids snickered, but it made my blood boil. Before I knew it, I stepped forward and called out, "Take it easy, Coach, he's trying his best."

It was stupid to do, just that I found that out quite too late. Mr. Simmons spun around, surprised that anyone had spoken back. "What did you say?" he demanded, eyes narrowing.

I swallowed. My heart was pounding, but I stood my ground. "I just... I think he's doing his best, sir," I repeated, a bit more quietly.

Mr. Simmons's jaw tightened. "That so? How about you take five laps for him, since you're so eager to speak up?" He blew the whistle sharply. "Everyone, hit the locker room. Except you," he pointed at me. "You stay and run."

I ran those five laps around the gym alone, under Coach's hard stare. When I finally finished, Coach Simmons simply said, "Detention. After school. Maybe that'll teach you when to keep your mouth shut."

It didn't feel fair - I was defending someone - but I nodded and went to shower, my face burning. Later, in detention (my first ever), I sat scribbling lines about respect and authority, feeling more angry than ashamed. Mom was furious when she heard I'd gotten in trouble, but once I explained why, her expression softened. She still made me write an apology letter to Coach Simmons and to the boy I tried to defend, insisting that I could have handled it without talking back disrespectfully. I begrudgingly did it, understanding her point. But a part of me was proud I hadn't just watched silently.

Another time, in the cafeteria, a one-year senior thought it'd be hilarious to stand behind a heavier girl in our class and moo loudly as she walked by with her lunch tray. A couple of his buddies chuckled, but many of us just froze in discomfort. The girl's face crumpled, her eyes fixed on the floor. Something in me snapped. I would never still get to understand the theory of mischief. What exactly was the benefiting in spiting someone else and making cheap jokes of it?

"Hey, cut it out," I barked across the table. The words burst out louder than I intended, echoing under the clatter of lunch hour. The mooing boy turned to me with a smirk.

"You got a problem?" he challenged, clearly not expecting anyone to confront him. He was taller and known to be a loudmouth, but I didn't care.

"Yeah," I shot back, standing up. My heart was doing that thumping thing again, but anger pushed me on. "With all that bull coming out of your mouth, you're the one acting like a cow."

A hush fell over the nearby tables, followed by a ripple of "ooohh!" from some onlookers. The smirk vanished off the boy's face as a red flush crept up his neck. For a second, I wondered if I'd just made everything worse. But then, unexpectedly, a couple of people snorted laughter. The corner of the girl's mouth twitched in a faint, appreciative smile as she hurried past.

"You think you're funny?" the boy muttered at me, trying to recover his dignity.

I shrugged, not breaking eye contact. "Think you owe her an apology."

We stared each other down for a moment. He didn't apologize - maybe that was too much to hope for - but he also didn't have a comeback. Instead, he grabbed his tray and slunk to another table, cheeks burning as everyone watched.

I sat back down, my hands trembling under the table. My friends stared at me like I'd grown a second head, then broke into grins. One clapped me on the back and others started joking about the look on that jerk's face. I just poked at my food, feeling a mix of triumph and anxiety. I hadn't planned to humiliate him; the words just flew out. But it shut him up and, more importantly, spared that girl further torment. In the back of my mind, I heard Mom's voice reminding me to be kind. I figured kindness sometimes meant standing between someone and cruelty.

Each instance was a risk; I could have easily become the next target for ridicule or retaliation. But more often than not, I walked away with a bit more self-assurance. People knew not to push me in certain ways. Not because I was intimidating; I wasn't; but because I had a reputation for not backing down from what I felt was right and God knows it took forever to build.

## Experiences Within A Team

Still, for every time I held my own, there were moments that reminded me I was "the boy without a dad." One came a few months into sophomore year. I had started playing on the JV basketball team and even got a few chances to suit up for varsity games. Basketball was my passion; not just because I loved the sport, but because it gave me a sense of belonging. Our team was like a rough-around-the-edges brotherhood. We sweated through drills together, celebrated wins, and consoled each other in losses. But even there, I couldn't escape reminders of what I lacked.

At one home game, a tightly contested match that came down to the wire, I sank a buzzerbeating shot from the corner. The gym erupted. My teammates swarmed me, the crowd in the bleachers (small as it was) went wild. It was the kind of moment I had dreamed about; the kind that plays out in slow-motion on highlight reels. As I emerged from the huddle of cheering teammates, grinning ear to ear, my eyes instinctively searched the stands for my mother. She was easy to find; she'd come straight from work still in her scrubs, and was standing up clapping with pride written all over her face. Our eyes met and she gave me the thumbs-up and a little celebratory fist pump. I beamed.

After we changed out of our jerseys, Mom found me outside the locker room. She wrapped me in a hug, sweaty as I was, not caring one bit. "I'm so proud of you," she whispered, and kissed the top of my head (to the great embarrassment of a couple teammates nearby, who snickered). I chuckled and gently pulled away. "Mo-om," I groaned in mock protest. But I hugged her back just as tight. I remember catching our coach watching us for a moment; Coach Simmons, a tall, stern man with a soft spot for his players. He had a peculiar look on his face, something between admiration for my mom's dedication and a touch of sadness. Maybe he was thinking what I was thinking. On the drive home that night, Mom chattered excitedly about the game; she always tried to learn the terminology and mimic the commentary, which both amused and touched me; and I felt a swell of gratitude.

It wasn't long before Coach Simmons himself became something of a near-father figure to me. He wasn't the easiest man to play for; he demanded discipline, had zero tolerance for disrespect, and pushed us hard in practice; but he was fair and fiercely protective of his team. One afternoon, after a minor scuffle broke out during practice between two players, Coach blew his whistle and made us all line up on the baseline. We expected a lecture or some punitive sprints, but instead he went down the line, looking each of us in the eye. When he reached me, he paused. "You've got a good head on your shoulders," he said quietly so only I could hear. Then louder, to everyone, "We're a family. Start acting like one. That means no fighting. You got each other's backs, on and off the court. Understood?" We all nodded, chastened.

Later that season, I had a one-on-one conversation with Coach that stuck with me. I'd been struggling to balance academics and sports, pulling a couple of late nights to finish projects after away games. One day I must have dozed off in history class because the teacher informed Coach, and he called me into his office. I sat there, nervous, as he closed the door. His small office was cluttered with play diagrams and had a faint smell of old sweat and coffee.

"You know why you're here," he started. I nodded, staring at my sneakers. I expected a reprimand or maybe a warning that if my grades slipped, I'd be benched (our school was strict about that). But instead, Coach leaned forward on his elbows. "How's everything at home?" he asked, not unkindly.

The question caught me off guard. "Uh... fine," I mumbled. "Mom's on me about my homework and stuff."

He cleared his throat. "Listen, I know it's just your mom raising you, right?" He looked a little uncomfortable even mentioning it. I tensed, bracing for pity or some clichéd talk about "manning up."

"Yes, sir," I said cautiously.

Coach gave a thoughtful nod. "She doing okay? Working a lot, I bet."

"Yeah. Night shifts mostly, but she's always... she makes it work," I said, unsure why my heart was thumping. It felt odd discussing Mom with him.

A small smile touched his lips. "She's a strong woman. I see her at every game, cheering louder than anyone." That made me smile too, despite my nerves. "Look," he continued, "the reason I asked you in isn't to get on your case. It's to tell you I understand it's not easy doing all this without a father at home. I want you to know that if you ever need anything; advice, someone to talk to, whatever; my door's open. You hear?"

I looked up, meeting his eyes. There was no pity there, just sincerity. For a moment I couldn't find my voice. This was a man who barked at us to run faster, who stomped his feet when we missed layups; now awkwardly offering me a lifeline of support. It meant more to me than I could express. "Thank you, Coach," I managed softly.

He gave a gruff nod and leaned back, shifting back into his usual tone. "Alright. Now, about you sleeping in class; knock that off. Good grades, good game. That's the deal."

"Yes, sir," I replied, smiling.

I left his office feeling ten feet tall; not because anything dramatic had changed, but because in Coach's own brusque way, he showed he cared. He saw me, the whole me, and wasn't counting me out or treating me as fragile because of my family situation. If anything, he expected more from me, knowing the load I carried. That was a form of respect that made me determined to deliver.

Encounters like that, with Coach and others, filled in bits of the puzzle that Mom alone couldn't. Coach taught me about commitment and standing up for your people. Mr. Thompson, my English teacher (and now mentor in the writing club I'd finally joined junior year), nurtured my voice and often reminded me that vulnerability can be its own kind of strength. And then there was Mr. Jenkins, our elderly neighbour. He took it upon himself to teach me a few classic "manly" skills that; truth be told; Mom or I might have figured out via trial and error, but it felt nice to learn from him. There were so many others that stood as representative figures through the journey to manhood; it needs a dedicated chapter to it which I'll be narrating afterwards.

## Social Night Eventualities

One chilly Saturday, I was struggling to get a knot right on a tie for the winter formal dance. I had a thrifted suit jacket and a tie Mom bought on sale, and I was determined to show up looking sharp. But after twenty minutes of standing in front of the mirror with my tongue out, the tie looked like a mangled ribbon. Mom tried to assist (she rarely had to wear ties, obviously, but had seen a few YouTube tutorials), yet we still couldn't get it right. I was getting frustrated and anxious; picking up my date in half an hour; when a knock came at our door. It was Mr. Jenkins from down the hall, leaning on his cane and grinning. He had been one of the reasons I began playing basketball, switching from soccer after our constant practice together in his yard. He was much older now and we had stopped our little trainings especially now that he depended on the cane.

"Heard some colourful language coming from this direction. Need a hand?" he chuckled. He had apparently heard my exasperated outburst through our thin apartment walls and came to investigate. Sheepishly, I admitted defeat and asked for help. With a deftness that belied his age, he looped the tie around my neck and talked me through the steps; the same way his father had shown him, he said. As he worked, he gave a gentle pat to my shoulder. "Your mom's done a fine job with you. She really has," he said quietly so only I could hear, as Mom was in the other room fetching her camera. "You make sure to thank her."

"I will, sir," I replied honestly. I looked in the mirror; Mr. Jenkins had fashioned a perfect Windsor knot. I stood a little straighter, looking every bit a young man ready for his dance. Before he left, I managed to say, "Thank you... for, you know, everything." He just smiled and waved it off, but I hoped he understood I meant more than just the tie. Life was moving quite speedily in those days and in no time, I wasn't going to have the chance to express that gratitude towards him anymore...

Anyway, armed with a proper tie and my mother's gentle reminders to "always be a gentleman," I headed out to pick up my date, palms sweating and heart racing. When I arrived at my date's house, her dad opened the door and sized me up; warmly, yet with a protective air. He shook my hand; a firm, quick grip; and joked, "You take good care of my little girl tonight." I assured him I would. The exchange was brief, but as I escorted my date to the car (Mom waiting at the curb to drive us), I felt a tiny pang of envy.

When we got to the school gym, I opened the car door for my date just as Mom had instructed and remembered to compliment her sparkly blue dress. Inside the dance, I tried my best to channel the polite confidence Mom had instilled in me. I noticed some of my friends showing off or cracking crude jokes to impress their dates; the kind of behavior that made the girls roll their eyes. I decided I was better off simply being respectful and attentive. Maybe being raised by a woman had given me a bit of insight, because by the end of the night my date was laughing at my corny jokes and thanking me for "being such a sweet guy." I couldn't wait to tell Mom that her advice had paid off.

## Everybody Has a Bad Day

Not everything was rosy, of course. I had my setbacks and screw-ups like any teenager. I recall one game in particular where I lost my cool. It was an away game, and I'd been in a foul mood from the start after arguing with Mom that morning about missing curfew the night before. My head wasn't in the best place. In the fourth quarter, with the score tight, I drove to the hoop and felt a hard slap on my arm; a clear foul; but the referee's whistle stayed silent. Frustration flared hot in my chest.

Without thinking, I slammed the basketball on the court. "Are you blind?!" I shouted at the ref in reflex, the words echoing through the gym. Damn, everyone turned to me. The ref's face turned stony as he blew his whistle twice and signalled a technical foul. Coach Simmons was on his feet in an instant, eyes blazing. He yanked me out of the game, and I spent the final minutes on the bench, head in my hands, as we ended up losing by a narrow margin.

The locker room was silent afterward. I felt the weight of my teammates' disappointment and my own shame pressing down on me. On the bus ride home, no one spoke to me; not out of anger, but because they knew I knew I had messed up. I slumped in my seat, replaying that moment of lost temper again and again. By the time we pulled into our school parking lot, I wanted to melt into the floor.

I expected Coach to tear into me once we were alone, but he didn't. He just looked at me long and hard and said, 'Everybody has a bad day. What matters is how you fix it.' That was it... At practice the next day, before Coach even said anything, I stepped forward and apologized to the team for letting my temper get the best of me. As penance, I led the entire squad in our suicide drills, running myself ragged... I approached the referee (who had come to oversee our scrimmage) and offered a sincere apology for my outburst.

By our next game, the incident was behind us. We still lost - yes, because life was not a silk bed with sprinkled roses. It didn't mean the lesson wasn't learnt though. Senior year rolled around faster than I expected. I found myself one of the older kids, a quasi-mentor to younger players and underclassmen in the clubs I was in. I noticed that some freshmen and sophomores would come to me for advice; about classes, dealing with teachers, even handling bullies. Apparently, my reputation for speaking up had made the rounds. I took this role seriously, remembering how much it meant when older peers or adults had guided me. I tried to be that steady presence for them. It felt good, and it also kept me grounded and out of trouble (hard to act too foolish when you know others are looking up to you).

## Coming Into My Own

One of the biggest tests of my character came during a city-wide basketball tournament in the spring of senior year. By then, I was co-captain of the team. We fought our way to the finals, a big game at a college arena downtown; the largest venue I'd ever played in. The pressure was immense. A few college scouts were rumoured to be attending, and for some of my teammates this was make-or-break for scholarships. My mom was there in the stands, having traded shifts to get the day off. She had even, I suspect, coordinated with a few of my friends' dads to have them keep an extra eye on me and the team. She'd become friendly with many of them over the years at games, and while none overstepped, I often got an encouraging clap on the back from them (which I secretly appreciated).

In that game, we played our hearts out, every one of us leaving sweat on that court. In the final minute, we were trailing by a single point. I remember with just seconds left, I drove hard toward the basket and drew the defence, then dished the ball to our center, who scored just as the buzzer sounded. We'd done it; we won by one.

The explosion of cheers was deafening. My teammates lifted the center in the air, everyone jumping and hugging like little kids. I was caught in the happy chaos when I spotted one

of our opposing players collapsed on the floor, head in his hands. He was their star, and he'd played a hell of a game. In the middle of our celebration, I felt an odd tug at my conscience. It was the kind of moment where one could easily get lost in victory and forget everything else. But I broke from our huddle and walked over to him. I extended a hand down. He looked up, eyes wet; whether from tears or sweat I couldn't tell, maybe both. After a heartbeat, he took my hand and I pulled him up. "You played great, man," I shouted over the noise, and patted his shoulder. He gave me a tight nod, managing a "You too."

It was a little gesture; one I had not even taken any value in until I would later realize coach had been watching when he told me that single act impressed him more than any shot I made. For me, it just felt natural, maybe because Mom had always taught me empathy, or because I'd been on the other side of disappointment plenty of times.

*Winning with dignity was just as important as losing with it.*

After the trophy presentation and photos (Mom elbowed her way to the front of the parent paparazzi to snap a dozen pictures), we all headed out. As I was leaving the arena, a familiar voice called my name. It was Darius; the same Darius from the cafeteria as I would later get to discover his name. He had graduated the year prior and I hadn't seen him since. Turns out he'd come to watch the tournament and was hanging around with some other alumni. I braced inwardly, unsure of how that memory sat with him. But to my relief, he walked up grinning, clapped me on the back and said, "Heard you're doing good things, man. That was a solid game. Congrats."

"Thanks, D," I replied, the old tension truly gone. As he walked off, I realized time had worked a strange alchemy. We weren't friends, but any animosity had faded. Maybe it was just maturity, or maybe I had finally earned a bit of respect in his eyes too; not through intimidation or fear, but by coming into my own.

A few weeks later, I stood in a stiff graduation gown, sweating in the late spring sun along with a hundred other seniors. Graduation day; the culmination of four tumultuous, transformative years. We sat in neat rows on the football field, the principal droning through speeches, while my mind replayed highlight reels of high school: the laughter, the fights, the late-night study sessions, the quiet talks with mentors, the cheers of the crowd, the silence of the library. And in every scene, somewhere, the figure of my mother; cheering, listening, waiting up, pushing me onward. I glanced into the stands and found her, as always, a beacon. She was sitting among other families, but somehow, in that moment, it felt like just her and me. She waved enthusiastically when I caught her eye. I gave a small wave back, then quickly put my hand down, embarrassed, as my friends chuckled. But I didn't really mind. The younger me would have wished to be swallowed up by the ground.

When my name was called and I walked across the stage, I shook the principal's hand and accepted the diploma scroll. It felt weighty in my grip; symbolic not just of academic completion, but of every hurdle overcome to get here. As I moved my tassel from one side of my cap to the other, I felt a surge of emotion I hadn't expected. I looked out again at the audience. Amid the clapping, there was an emptiness where I wished my father could have been. I allowed myself to feel that for just a beat; that subtle ache. But then my gaze found Mom once more. She was clapping wildly, tears glinting on her cheeks. And right beside her was Coach Simmons, and Mr. Thompson, and even old Mr. Jenkins, all on their feet for me. Unbeknownst to me, Mom had invited them as her guests. In that beautiful, heart-stopping moment, I understood that while one chair in my life would forever remain unfilled, many others had slid into place around it.

After the ceremony, Mom enveloped me in an embrace that seemed to last forever. "I'm so, so proud of you," she kept saying, her voice muffled as she cried into my shoulder. I hugged her back, murmuring, "We did it." Because it was we. It had always been we. Coach came up and gave me a firm handshake and a rare smile. Mr. Thompson handed me a signed copy of a favourite novel as a graduation gift, with a note encouraging me to keep writing. Mr. Jenkins patted my cheek lightly and joked I was making him feel old.
Surrounded by this patchwork family, I felt an overwhelming wave of gratitude wash over me.

It was the best feeling!

# CHAPTER 5

# MIRRORS & SHADOWS

One of my earliest "borrowed" father figures was Grandpa - Mom's father, and though he was an unforgettable man, he was hardly really around and we got to see only once in a while as he soon had to retire to constant medical care alongside Grandma under health circumstances that hurt so badly, I don't even discuss them.

The little times we met were profound; memories I will cherish to my grave. As a young child, I had almost mistaken him for my very own father. He was much stronger then before the illness struck. So by the time I was old enough to begin navigating my life, he was much farther away but anytime I remember I knew how to fish or hold a shaving stick and had a weird taste for the 1900s music, I'd remember it was all Grandpa. The holiday where he taught me to shave at thirteen would be the last time I saw him healthy and strong enough. Then the moment before I went for college. After then, it just went down a rabbit hole of quiet, sad memories as he and Grandma *slowly left us... for good.*

## Mr. Thompson

In the absence of a father, another early father figure was Mr. Thompson, as you've met him briefly. The earlier chapters have only brushed the surface to how deeply this man was an influence so he probably deserves a section in a chapter.

He was a tall, even-tempered man with kind eyes behind wire-framed glasses. In a school full of chaos and noise, Mr. Thompson's classroom was an oasis of calm. He had a way of making every student feel seen and heard - especially me. I still remember the afternoon he pulled me aside after class. I had drawn a picture of my family for an assignment, and it was just my mother and me on the page. "You have a real talent for drawing, James," he said softly, squatting down to meet my eyes. "And a real love for your mom, I can see that. You took such care drawing her smile." I was surprised he noticed these details. Many teachers would have just pinned the picture on a wall and moved on, but Mr. Thompson wanted to talk about it.

Curious yet cautious, I admitted that I liked art and that my mom was my hero. Mr. Thompson nodded as if this was the most important information in the world. "She sounds like a special lady," he replied. "You know, it's okay to feel proud of her and also wish you had... well, more." His voice was gentle, and I understood he meant a father. He remains one of the earliest people to decipher the longing in me and actually do something kind about it.

Over the weeks that followed, Mr. Thompson became more than just a teacher; he became a mentor. He lent me books from his personal shelf - stories of young men overcoming struggles, classic novels with heroes and their guiding figures. After I devoured each one, he'd ask me questions about the characters as if trying to get me to articulate my own thoughts on what makes a good man. We'd sit during lunch or after school, discussing courage, integrity, and empathy without ever labelling the conversations as such. It was such subtle form of learning; one where you don't even notice you're learning so you never grow weary. At the time, I simply enjoyed the attention and the feeling of having a man take interest in me and my ideas. In hindsight, I realize he was gently equipping me with a moral vocabulary, giving me words and concepts to understand the kind of man I wanted to grow into.

I wasn't the only kid Mr. Thompson mentored, but he had a way of making me feel uniquely valued. Once, when I got a B+ on a math test I'd struggled with, he patted my shoulder and said, "I knew you could do it if you kept at it." It was just a simple encouragement, but coming from him it felt significant - like I had made him proud. I basked in that feeling. Mr. Thompson's pride was something I felt I had earned, and that made it shine all the brighter. In those moments, he was a mirror for me and looking back at it now, I consider him a reflection of patience, kindness, and the steady confidence of a man who knew himself and wanted to bring out the best in others. I remember thinking, *If I could be like him, I'd be doing alright.*

I didn't realize at the time that not every mentor would stay in my life forever. When I finished sixth grade, I was crushed to learn Mr. Thompson was moving, but we kept in touch via letters for a while, his steady voice guiding me until life eventually pulled us apart. This made it all the better when Mom got him to come for my high school graduation...

## Coach Simmons

One evening after practice, I stayed late to shoot free throws alone. Coach Simmons emerged from his office and walked over, rebounding the ball as it slipped through the hoop. He tossed it back to me and said,

*"You've got talent, kid, but talent only takes you so far. You got to work twice as hard when you've got half as much support at home. It isn't fair, but it's the truth."*

His blunt honesty startled me. He wasn't cruel about it, just stating a fact: I didn't have a dad to drive me to practice early or help me with drills in the driveway, a least until Mr. Jenkins couldn't help anymore. My mom did what she could, but between double shifts at the hospital and keeping our lives together, she couldn't be on the sidelines of every practice. Coach Simmons looked me in the eye. There was no pity there - just a challenge. "I'm here to help if you're willing to put in the work. You coming tomorrow morning? 6 AM?"

I hesitated. Mom wouldn't be able to drive me that early, and I mumbled as much. Coach Simmons just nodded. "I drive right by your apartment complex on my way here. I'll pick you up. But only if you're serious about getting better. Are you serious, son?"

He called me *son*.

That word hung in the air for a moment, electrifying and strange. No man had ever called me that before. I guess back then, I was definitely overreacting as it wasn't uncommon to find elderly men referencing young boys that way but back then at that moment, it meant something more to me.

I stood up a bit taller, swallowing the lump in my throat. "Yes, Coach. I'm serious." True to his word, Coach Simmons was outside my building the next morning, engine idling at 5:45 AM. He didn't honk - he just waited, knowing I'd be watching for him. I slipped out the door into the predawn chill, and we drove to the gym as the sky lightened. Those early morning sessions were gruelling; he made me run drills until my legs burned and practice shots until my arms ached. But he was there alongside me, rebounding, correcting my form, pushing me beyond what I thought my limits were. In those quiet moments before the rest of the team arrived, he also shared bits of his own life - how he'd been raised by a single mother too, how a coach had once done the same favour for him. "I wouldn't be here today if not for the people who guided me," he told me one morning as I collapsed on the bench after a particularly hard drill. "*So I expect you to pay attention and give it your all. Then one day, you'll pass it on to someone else. That's how you thank those who help you - by helping the next person in line.*"

In his gruff way, Coach Simmons was telling me that being a man meant both accepting help and giving it when you have the chance. It struck me that his tough-love drills were a form of care. He wanted to see me grow, not just as an athlete but as a person. At a point, I had to consider the similarities between the both of us and wonder if I'd end up like him - gruff and tough. I guess as life went on, I realized I wouldn't.

Between Mr. Thompson and Coach Simmons, I was blessed with two strong mirrors reflecting positive qualities: patience, kindness, determination, generosity. Each of them, in his own style, showed me pieces of the puzzle that is manhood. I collected those pieces eagerly, trying to assemble an image of what it meant to "be a man." But even as I gathered these shining examples, I couldn't escape the other figures in my world - the ones who cast long shadows across my path. The truth was, not all the men I looked up to turned out to be worthy of admiration.

Some offered a conflicting vision of manhood: a version loud with bravado but lacking substance, full of strength but void of tenderness. As I entered my early teens, I often felt torn between the lessons of the good men in my life and the allure of those who walked a darker road.

## The Allure of Shadows

In my neighbourhood, there were older boys and men whose lives seemed to orbit on the edge of trouble. To a fatherless kid hungry for male influence, some of these figures held a strange allure. They projected confidence and toughness, and they got respect - not the kind you earn from kindness or achievement, but the kind of fearful respect that comes with intimidation. I could see that people - kids and even some adults - stepped aside when these guys walked past. They wore their toughness like armor. And in a world where I sometimes felt vulnerable, that armor looked appealing.

One of these figures was a teenager named Damon who lived a few blocks away. Damon was about seventeen, a few years older than me, and he had a reputation. He wasn't the biggest or strongest guy around, but he carried himself with a swagger that made people believe he was dangerous to cross. I'd often see him and his crew at the outdoor basketball court in our complex, dominating the court not just with skill but with taunts and a flashy style that made all the little kids stare wide-eyed. He was quick to laugh but just as quick to anger. More than once, I'd seen him shove someone who annoyed him or heard about him roughing up a kid who dared to challenge him in a game.

At first, I watched Damon from a distance, equal parts admiring and wary. I was about thirteen when he first spoke to me. I was dribbling a ball on the side of the court, waiting for my turn to play, when he sauntered over. "You playin', shorty?" he asked. His tone was hard to read - half-teasing, half-threatening. Plus, those weren't exactly some polite choices of words, but anyway... I nodded, suddenly self-conscious about my age and size.
"I've seen you around. Coach Simmons' boy, right?" He said it with a slight smirk, the word boy hanging in the air. I didn't like the way he said it, as if being guided by a coach was something to mock, but I also felt a rush of pride that he'd noticed me at all.

"Yeah, I play on the school team," I responded, trying to sound confident. Damon exchanged a glance with one of his friends and then tossed me the ball unexpectedly. I nearly fumbled it, which made his crew snicker. "Show me what you got," he challenged. I hesitated only a second before driving toward the hoop, attempting a layup around him.
He was faster than he looked - he stripped the ball from me easily and laughed as I stumbled. "That all Coach Simmons teach you? Gotta be tougher than that, little man!" I flushed with embarrassment and a prick of anger. They were teasing, but there was an edge to it.

Over the next few months, I found myself crossing paths with Damon and his crew more often. Sometimes they'd let me join their pick-up games if they needed an extra body. I learned quickly that on their court, skill mattered less than showing no fear. If you complained about a foul, they'd laugh you off. If you got knocked down, you got up quick and acted like it didn't hurt. It was a kind of toughness test, and I was determined to prove myself. Part of me knew Coach Simmons would disapprove of me hanging around them -these weren't exactly the disciplined student-athletes he tried to mould us into. But another part of me was drawn in by the energy, the bravado, the freedom with which they lived. They skipped school without a worry, talked back to whoever they pleased, and seemed to make their own rules. To a kid who spent his life trying to do everything right, their way of living was like looking at the world turned upside down. It was wrong, I knew deep down, but it looked exciting.

## Two Conflicting Figures

By the time I turned fourteen, I felt like I was living in two worlds. At school and basketball practice, I had structure and guidance. But after school, out on the streets or at the park, I sometimes stepped into that other world - the one ruled by different laws. Damon and his friends valued things like loyalty to the crew, showing no weakness, and demanding respect through fear or force. They weren't outright criminals (at least not yet), but they lived by a rough code. In their view, being a man meant you didn't let anyone mess with you, and you definitely didn't walk away from a challenge or insult. It was an eye for an eye, and sometimes an eye for a sideways look. This was the opposite of what I learned at home, where Mom would tell me, "Be the bigger person, James. Don't sink to their level," whenever I had conflicts at school. And Coach Simmons always hammered in, "Discipline.
Control. Don't let your temper make you stupid." He'd say that to any of us who got hotheaded on the court. Their advice was basically: *use your head, not your fists.* But for Damon's world? Damn, it glorified the fists!

I was usually good at keeping these worlds separate, sliding between them like I spoke two languages. With Coach and Mom, I was the respectful, driven kid. With Damon and the guys, I tried to be cool, unbothered, and street-smart. I didn't emulate their worst behaviours - I wasn't shoplifting from the corner store or smoking weed behind the building when they did. Often, I'd just stand by, heart hammering, as a lookout of sorts, never brave enough to fully join yet not strong enough to walk away. I rationalized that I was just hanging out, that I wasn't doing anything bad myself. But I knew, deep down, that I was inching closer to a line.

That line finally got crossed one afternoon in a way that jolted me awake. It started with something almost innocent: a one-on-one basketball challenge. Damon loved to call out younger players to boost his own rep - he'd beat them with ease and laugh, establishing his dominance on the court. That day, he was strutting around after winning a game, and one of my classmates, Kevin, muttered something under his breath. Kevin was a quiet kid, not very athletic, and I was surprised to even see him at the court, although we played together every now and then which had led to the moment I shattered Mrs. Candice's window. Maybe he came looking for me, or maybe he was just passing by. But Damon heard the mutter - something like "It's easy to win when you foul on every play." It was true; Damon played dirty and everyone knew it. But you didn't say it.

In a flash, Damon was in Kevin's face, towering over him. Kevin looked scared and tried to backpedal, but two of Damon's friends blocked his way, smirking. I was off to the side, frozen, clutching my basketball. My stomach dropped. I knew this pattern: someone would make Damon lose face, and Damon would make them pay for it. Usually with his fists.

"What did you say, little man?" Damon hissed. Kevin stammered, "N-nothing. I didn't say anything." Damon shoved him hard in the chest. Kevin stumbled back into one of the other guys, who pushed him back toward Damon like a ping-pong ball. "Sounded like you were accusing me of somethin'," Damon insisted, voice dangerously low. "You calling me a cheater?"

Kevin's eyes were wide. "No, I just - "

Of course, he was a cheater, and the thing with people that didn't earn their prizes honestly was that they felt threatened at the slightest hint of an accusation. Without thinking, I stepped forward. "Hey, Damon, chill. He's nobody, man, he's just leaving." I said it as calmly as I could, trying to sound like I was on Damon's side even as I planted myself between him and Kevin. My heart was pounding so hard I thought I might faint. Damon turned his sharp gaze to me. "Stay out of this, James," he warned. "This ain't got nothing to do with you." Kevin looked at me, silently pleading for help.

For a second, I thought Damon might actually back off. He stared at me, surprised. Then came the sneer. "Or what, James? You gonna make me?" The guys around us chuckled darkly. My palms were sweaty, but I didn't move. I had visions of Coach Simmons dragging me off the court for what I was about to do, of Mom's disappointed face, of Mr. Thompson shaking his head. But I also saw Kevin out of the corner of my eye, terrified and fragile in the way I often felt but tried hard not to show. Something in me couldn't walk away.

When Damon swung, I wasn't ready. His fist connected with my cheek and an explosion of pain shot through my face. I stumbled, the world tilting. It was the first time I'd ever been punched for real. Coach's drills and sports scrapes were nothing compared to this fire that burst along my cheekbone. I heard Kevin yelp and a chorus of "Ooooh!" from the spectators. Damon was on me before I could recover, grabbing my shirt. Instinct kicked in - I swung back, wildly, my fist slamming into his shoulder. It only made him angrier. He drove me backwards and we went down in a heap, scrabbling in the dust beside the court.

I could hear shouting - some of the onlookers were chanting, "Fight! Fight!" It was chaos and noise and adrenaline. Damon was stronger, but I was fuelled by a righteous anger and the desperation of defending not just Kevin, but maybe myself too - defending that vulnerable kid inside me who was sick of being afraid. I caught Damon on the jaw at one point, and he hissed a curse. He managed to pin me for a moment, his forearm against my throat. I clawed at his arm, gasping, my vision blurring. In that split second, the world slowed: I thought of my mother. I thought of how devastated she'd be if I came home bruised and bleeding, or worse, if I didn't come home at all because something went horribly wrong. The thought gave me a surge of strength - or maybe it was just blind panic. I heaved to the side and we rolled.

Suddenly, hands were pulling us apart. It was Mr. Toby, the community center director who also helped coach our team occasionally. In all the commotion, none of us had seen him approach. "That's enough!" he barked, positioning himself between me and Damon with an authority that neither of us dared to challenge. I was panting, chest heaving, dust stinging my eyes. Damon wiped a trickle of blood from his split lip, eyes still furious but now a little uncertain. Mr. Toby was older, in his fifties, but still fit and with that nononsense stance of a former athlete. He glared at all of us. "This how you kids settle things? Like animals?" He shook his head in disappointment. "Damon, take your boys and get out of here. Now. And if I see you lay a hand on anyone around here again, you'll be banned from the center and the court, you hear me?"

Damon spat on the ground and muttered something under his breath, but he jerked his head for his friends to follow. He shot me a look - not exactly of remorse, more like this isn't over - but he turned and left. The circle of spectators disintegrated quickly, everyone suddenly remembering they had somewhere else to be now that the show was over. Kevin stood off to the side, trembling and wiping tears from his face. Mr. Toby sighed and looked at me. "You okay, James?" he asked, and his tone held both concern and a tinge of *I expected better from you.*

I'll never forget what happened next, though.

Mr. Toby walked me the few blocks back to my apartment. At first, we were silent. I was limping a little - Damon had kicked my leg at some point - and I could feel the bruise blooming on my face. I was terrified of what Mom would say, but also still angry, mostly at myself. Finally, Mr. Toby cleared his throat.

"You want to tell me what that was all about?" he asked. I didn't, really, but the explanation tumbled out: how Damon was picking on Kevin, how I tried to intervene. With each word, I expected him to chide me for fighting. But he just listened. When I finished, he put a hand on my shoulder, gentle despite his earlier anger. "Standing up for your classmate, huh. That took guts, James."

"You've got some awkward choices of who to respect." He shrugged. "but fighting... look where it got you." We reached my building and stopped by the stairwell. "There are better ways to handle things. You know that. You've got good people teaching you better ways."

I nodded, tears of frustration pricking my eyes.

I didn't know how to finish. Mr. Toby sighed. "When you try to be reasonable around some people, they just won't listen, period. Doesn't mean you lower yourself to their level. You gotta be smarter. You're better than that."

There it was again - that echo of what Mom always said, what Coach drilled into us. *Be the bigger person. Don't let your temper make you stupid.* Hearing it from Mr. Toby, who I respected, hit hard. He wasn't yelling or scolding me in front of others; he was just talking to me man to man, as if I were already one.

Before he left, Mr. Toby squeezed my shoulder once. "Heal up, and I better see you at the center tomorrow. We've got that tournament coming up. You don't want Simmons throwing in salt on those injuries when he hears of this."

I managed a small smile and said, "Yes, sir."

That night I made a silent vow to be more discerning about who I looked to for guidance. I had seen up close the difference between a mirror and a shadow. A mirror like Coach or Mr. Thompson cared about my future; a shadow like Damon cared only about the moment, about himself. One would help me build myself up, the other could only tear me - or someone else - down.

I finally understood what he meant. In your journey, there will be mirrors and shadows. The mirrors were there, shining light on the path, and you must make a choice, to follow the reflection of yourself in those good images, or be lost in the hollow of a shadow.

# CHAPTER 6

# A MOTHER'S BURDEN, A SON'S AWEARNESS

One of my earliest memories of Mom's double duty is from when I was about seven years old. It was a late evening, long past my bedtime. I remember waking up thirsty and padding out of my room to get a glass of water. The apartment was mostly dark, but a sliver of light glowed from the kitchen. There was Mom, still in her light blue nurse's scrubs, sitting at the small table with her head in her hands. A half-eaten sandwich and a pile of papers (which I would later realize were bills) were in front of her. She was so still and quiet that at first, I thought maybe she was asleep. I stood there watching and after a moment, she lifted her head and I saw her face. Her eyes were closed and her cheeks were damp. She was crying silently.

It was the first time I'd ever seen my mother cry.

To me, she had always been invincible - the fixer of broken cars and the vanquisher of nightmares. Seeing her in that vulnerable state felt wrong, like stumbling into a secret room I wasn't meant to enter. In the end, I backed away and crept to bed with a heart heavy with confusion. The next morning, she was back to her energetic self, but that moment established a kind of unspoken pact: she pretended she could do it all without breaking, and I pretended not to see the moments when she bent under the weight.

As I grew, her responsibilities only increased. She had to keep a roof over our heads, which meant long hours at the hospital. Often, she'd volunteer for overtime or double shifts because the extra pay meant we could catch up on rent or set a bit aside for a rainy day.

There were evenings when I'd do my homework sitting at a corner table in the hospital cafeteria because she couldn't find a sitter and didn't want to leave me home alone. The nurses all knew me by name, giving me chocolate milk cartons and cookies while I waited patiently. I'd see Mom rushing back and forth down the corridors, tending to her patients with endless patience. She'd pause occasionally to blow me a kiss or give a little wave. Those nights always ended the same way: with me curled up in a vinyl chair, dozing, until Mom finished her shift near midnight and gently guided me to the car for the ride home. I'd wake up the next morning to find her already up and moving, packing my lunch bleary eyed, fuelled by love, and maybe a little caffeine.

# Quiet Sacrifices

Some sacrifices that Mother made came in silent tones, like the basketball shoes I desired in my desperate act to fit in. Mine were third-hand and peeling, and I knew money was tight, but I was at that age where fitting in felt like life or death. Later that night, I overheard her talking to my Aunt Nia on the phone. Standing behind our thin living room wall, I listened as she said, "I hate that I can't even afford shoes for him without scraping.

I'm thinking of taking an extra shift this weekend..." Her voice was strained, laced with guilt and worry. My chest tightened; here I was upset about shoes, and there she was planning to work even more hours so I wouldn't feel left out. A week later, she had somehow saved up and took me to the store. I was elated to get those bright white sneakers, but later I found out she had worked a double shift and sold a piece of jewellery her mother had given her just to make up the cost. Nothing had made me feel dumber, but it never made Mom feel the effort was less worth it.

There were countless small sacrifices like that. Mom often skipped meals, claiming she wasn't hungry, when I suspected she was just making sure I had enough. If we had leftovers, she'd pack them neatly into my lunch for the next day, saying she'd grab something at work, though I doubted she had time to eat during her shifts. She wore the same winter coat for years. Remembering it now makes me laugh. It was a sturdy gray one that had seen better days. And she wore it so that I could have a new coat when I outgrew mine. When our old clunky television broke, she chose not to replace it, funnelling that money toward a laptop I needed for school.

"No shortcuts," she would say whenever I suggested that maybe we didn't have to do something the hard, frugal way. She took pride in paying for things honestly, in budgeting down to the penny, in fixing what was broken instead of buying new. It was her way of maintaining dignity and control in a life that could easily feel out of control.

I also began to see how she balanced being both mother and father to me in her parenting style. She could be nurturing and gentle when it came to patching up my scraped knees with a Winnie-the-Pooh bandage and a kiss but she could also be stern when necessary. If I stepped out of line or gave her attitude, as all kids do, she wouldn't hesitate to lay down the law.

"You break it, you fix it," as she'd always say if I damaged something or hurt someone's feelings, marching me through apologies or chores to make amends. She didn't believe in coddling me when it came to owning up to my mistakes.

*"I expect you to be a good man one day,"* she told me often. *"Not just a successful man, but a good one. Strong enough to do the right thing, even when it's hard."* Those words echoed within me, especially after the fight with Damon. I realized she wasn't just talking about not breaking lamps or toys but she meant if I broke

trust or broke someone's heart or made a mess of my life, it was on me to fix it if I could. And these were lessons that were about to change me forever. She was raising me to be accountable, likely because she had seen too many people (perhaps including my father) shirk their responsibilities.

## When a Child Sees the Strain

For much of my childhood, I only saw what Mom wanted me to see: her strength, her love, her constant presence. But aside the night I had seen her cry, as I became a teenager, there were moments where the curtain lifted and I caught a glimpse of the cost behind that presence. One such moment came when I was in eighth grade, during a school honors ceremony.

I had worked hard that year and managed to make the honor roll. The school was hosting a special evening event to award certificates to all the honor roll students, and parents were invited. I brought home the invitation, excited and proud. Mom promised she'd be there, even if she had to trade a shift. I could tell how proud she was; she even invited Grandpa and Aunt Nia to come.

The night of the ceremony, I sat on the stage with my classmates, scanning the audience eagerly. Aunt Nia was there, camera in hand, flashing me a thumb-up. Grandpa had come too, dressed in his Sunday best, beaming at me. But Mom's seat, right between them, was empty. The program was starting and a knot of worry tightened in my stomach. Aunt Nia gave me a small shrug and an encouraging smile that said, she'll be here, don't worry. But I did worry. My section of the alphabet was called, and I walked across the stage to get my certificate. I looked out and still no sign of Mom. Grandpa clapped loudly, and Aunt Nia snapped a picture, but I felt a hollow disappointment that threatened to swallow my pride.

After the ceremony, as people milled about congratulating their kids, I stood with Aunt Nia and Grandpa, trying to hide my glances toward the door. I was fighting back the sting of tears, telling myself she must have been held up at work, that it wasn't because she didn't care. I knew that logically, but my 14-year-old heart was crushed in that moment.

Then, just as we were about to leave, I heard someone call my name. I turned and saw Mom rushing in, still in her scrubs, a windbreaker thrown over them. Her hair was escaping its ponytail, and she was slightly out of breath. She looked around frantically until she spotted me. "James! Oh my God, I'm so sorry I'm late!" She came over and pulled me into a tight hug right in front of everyone. I was embarrassed and relieved and upset all at once.

"I tried to get here, but a patient complication came up last minute," she explained hurriedly, "I'm so sorry, baby." Her eyes were brimming with tears, and I realized with a jolt that she was afraid I thought she didn't care. The truth was, some small part of me had wondered that, even knowing better.

Still overwhelmed by emotion, I muttered, "It's okay, Mom. It's not a big deal." But my voice betrayed me, cracking slightly. She held my face in her hands, taking in the subtle hurt I couldn't hide.

"It is a big deal. I'm so proud of you," she whispered. She insisted on taking a picture of me with my certificate right there, under the fluorescent school gym lights, making Grandpa and Aunt Nia pose with us. I managed a smile, but inside I felt a confusing swirl of gratitude that she came at all and a lingering hurt that she'd missed my moment.

Lying in bed sometime around midnight, I woke to the sound of muffled voices. My room was next to the living area, and through the thin wall I could hear Mom talking to Aunt Nia, who had stayed over on our couch. I crept closer to the wall to listen.

Mom's voice was shaking. "...I feel terrible, Nia. I let him down. He won this award and I wasn't there to see him get it." She was crying; I could hear the tears in her words. "What kind of mother am I? I'm trying to be his mother and father, but I can't be in two places at once." There was a pause and I heard the soft sound of Aunt Nia comforting her.

"You're a damn good mother," Aunt Nia replied. "James knows that. He's just a kid; he was hurt, sure, but he'll understand. You're doing the best you can."

Mom let out a long, shaky sigh. "Sometimes I don't know if the best I can do is enough. He deserves... he deserves everything. A whole family. I'm so scared that all this - " her voice cracked - "all this weight, I can't carry it forever." I felt a tear roll down my own cheek as I listened. I had never heard her sound so despairing. Aunt Nia hushed her gently.

"Listen to me. You are not alone, okay? You've got me, and Dad, and you've got James.

That boy loves you more than anything. You're the world to him."

I pressed my hand over my mouth to stifle a sob. Hearing Mom doubt herself, thinking she wasn't enough for me, broke something inside me and filled it with resolve. I wanted to burst out of my room and tell her she was doing great, that I was the one who was sorry for being so moody earlier. But I felt... frozen.

Aunt Nia continued softly, not knowing I was listening. She murmured more words of comfort, reminding Mom of how well I was doing in school, how polite and "goodhearted" I was. She credited Mom for all of that. Eventually, their voices died down and I heard Aunt Nia preparing the couch for sleep. At that point, I felt gratitude, guilt, love, and a fierce protective instinct all at once.

The next morning, I quietly resolved to show her that I did see it, or at least that I was beginning to. When she woke me up for school, I wrapped my arms around her in an

unprompted hug.

"Thank you for everything, Mom," I murmured. She seemed taken aback, then smiled and hugged me back fiercely.

"Oh... kay... You're welcome, baby," she whispered, perhaps not knowing what specific

thing I was thanking her for. But it didn't matter; I meant *everything*.

## Lessons in Resilience and Gratitude

From then on, I paid more attention. I picked up on the subtle ways stress would creep into Mom's demeanour: how she'd sit down for "just a minute" after dinner and instantly fall asleep in the armchair, or how she'd sometimes stare at the calendar and bite her lip, calculating how to juggle my school events with her work schedule. I started pitching in more without being asked: doing the dishes, taking out the trash, even attempting to cook simple meals (some of which ended up burnt, but it's the thought that counts).

At first, she protested, saying, "You've got to focus on your studies; that's your job." But I saw the relief in her eyes when she realized the trash had been taken out or the laundry folded. I was determined not to be another weight on her shoulders. I wanted to be a support, however small, to show her that she wasn't in it alone, just as Aunt Nia had said.

Mom had a saying she'd picked up from Grandpa and the willow tree; one of the key lessons she gave me to live with:

*"We bend, but we don't break."*

Whenever times were tough, she'd repeat it like a mantra. When the car broke down and the repair bill came out of our rent money, when I got chickenpox and she had to miss work she couldn't afford to miss, when anything threatened to overwhelm her, she'd close her eyes, take a breath, and say, "We bend, but we don't break." I came to understand that bending meant being flexible and finding a way through, but not breaking meant never losing ourselves or our hope. She certainly bent with every challenge - sometimes I worried she would snap under the pressure, but she never did. Her resilience was like a steel spring: pushed to the limit, but always finding a way to bounce back.

Watching her navigate life taught me what real strength looked like. I saw that strength isn't loud or boastful. It's not about how many pounds you can lift or how much money you make or how intimidating you can be. Real strength is my mother dragging herself out of bed at 5 AM after four hours of sleep to make sure I had breakfast before school. It's her holding back her own tears so she can wipe mine and tell me things will be okay. It's working a twelve-hour shift on her feet, comforting sick children all day, and then coming home and asking me with genuine interest how my day was. Her kind of strength carried tenderness within it. Far from being a weakness, that tenderness was the source of her strength. She could have been hardened by our situation, but instead she remained soft where it mattered, never letting the world steal her warmth or her hope.

This had a profound effect on my own understanding of manhood and adulthood in general. Earlier, I had looked to men to teach me how to be a man, and they certainly taught me crucial lessons. But my mother, without being a man, taught me perhaps the most important lessons of all: that resilience and compassion are two sides of the same coin, that taking responsibility is a form of love, that gratitude can be a source of strength rather than a sign of weakness. I started to emulate her in small ways, internalizing her values. At school, I became more compassionate toward classmates who struggled, remembering how Mom always said, "*Everyone's carrying something* - be kind." When I thought about my future, I no longer fantasized just about being rich or strong or admired in the shallow ways; I thought about being dependable, being someone others could count on the way I counted on Mom.

Along with that growing admiration came a pang of guilt that never fully left me. No matter how well I did in school or on the court, no matter how many part-time jobs I took on as I got older to help with the bills, I couldn't change the fact that my mother's life was harder because of me. It's a heavy realization for a teenager: that your existence, as much as it brings someone joy, also brings them hardship. I remember when that realization first hit me fully. It was sophomore year of high school, and I'd stayed late for tutoring. I had neglected to tell Mom I'd be late coming home. She panicked when I didn't show up after school, and when I finally walked in the door, I found her on the phone with Aunt Nia, frantically discussing the last time anyone had seen me. The look of relief on her face quickly turned to anger born of fear.

"James, do you have any idea how worried I was?" she scolded, tears in her eyes. "I thought something happened to you!"

I apologized profusely and explained where I'd been. She pulled me into a hug, her anger melting into shaky sighs.

"Please," she said, "I need you to be safe. You're all I have."

That's when it really sank in: my well-being was everything to her. If I slipped even a little, if I got into trouble, got hurt, or strayed down a wrong path, not only would I suffer, but she would too, perhaps even more. It made me view my choices in a new light. Doing the right thing, succeeding in school, staying out of harm's way. It wasn't just for me, it was for her. And it was good if we really wanted to stay together.

My life was tied to my mother's in a profound way. Realizing that was both a burden and a powerful motivation; I was determined not to let all her sacrifices be in vain. I pushed for better grades, not just for myself but so she could proudly hang my honor roll certificates on the fridge. I found a part-time job at a local grocery store by junior year, and though she cried and refused to take my first

paycheck, I saw how much we needed it, and I was proud to give back in even the smallest measure. Through all these changes, our bond deepened. We became, in some ways, partners. I was still her son and she was still the parent, but we supported each other emotionally. On days I sensed she was especially tired or down, I'd sit with her after dinner and just talk. She kissed my forehead.
"I do, and I'm so thankful for that."

Then I went to college... And I was all alone.

# The Becoming

**"Life is not a having and a getting, but a being and a becoming."**
*- Matthew Arnold*

# CHAPTER 7

# THE MANIFESTO OF MANHOOD
# EARLY COLLEGE LIFE

The morning I left for college was bright and bittersweet. I sat at our small kitchen table, swirling a spoon in my oatmeal while Mom bustled about, her voice upbeat as she double-checked my packing list. I watched her hands tremble slightly as she set down a plate of eggs, a small tear quickly wiped from her cheek. "I always knew this day would come," she said softly. "This is what we've worked for." We shared a quiet, profound moment, our shared sense of something ending and something beginning hanging in the air.

Just as we loaded our old car, Aunt Nia and Grandpa arrived for a proper send-off. Aunt Nia pressed a bag of her famous chocolate chip cookies into my hands, and Grandpa, who had driven hours to surprise me, enveloped me in a bear hug. He handed me a small, wrapped gift, reminding me that if I could catch a fish, I could do anything. Surrounded by this loving circle, I felt the full weight of the goodbye. I hugged them fiercely, watching their figures - Aunt Nia dabbing her eyes, Grandpa raising a stoic salute - until they disappeared from view. Part of me felt like a little kid again, except this time there was no promise of coming home in the afternoon.

The drive to campus took a few hours. At first, Mom kept up a stream of chatter - reminding me about safe driving, balanced diets, and procrastination. As the cityscape gave way to rolling fields, a comfortable quiet fell between us. I reached over and gently squeezed her arm. She glanced at me, smiling softly, understanding the unspoken language that had always existed between us. She placed her free hand briefly over mine.

"Do you remember your first day of kindergarten?" Mom asked suddenly, eyes still on the road. I laughed.

"Vaguely. I remember you gave me that pep talk." She nodded. "I sat in the parking lot and cried for ten minutes before I drove to work. I knew you'd be fine, but it was the first time I had to let go a little."

My throat tightened. "I'll be fine, Mom," I said quietly.

"I know," she replied. "You're ready." The conviction in her voice eased some of my own doubts.

"Do you remember your first day of kindergarten?" Mom asked suddenly, eyes still on the road.

I let out a small laugh. "Vaguely. I remember you gave me that pep talk in the car, how making new friends might feel scary but everyone's nervous on the first day."

She nodded. "And you got out of the car with your little backpack, so brave. I sat in the parking lot and cried for ten minutes before I drove to work."

"You did?" I never knew that.

"Oh yes," she said, chuckling at the memory. "I knew you'd be fine. But it was the first time I had to let go a little." She paused, then continued with a tender tone, "This feels a lot like that day."

My throat tightened. "I'll be fine, Mom," I said quietly.

"I know," she replied. "You're ready." A simple statement, but the conviction in her voice eased some of my own doubts. If Mom believed I was ready, maybe I truly was.

We arrived at campus by early afternoon. The university was bustling with the controlled chaos of move-in day. Cars and SUVs crammed with dorm items crawled along the roads.
Upperclassmen in matching orientation t-shirts directed traffic and greeted families. My nerves reignited seeing clusters of students hugging their parents goodbye, excited voices mixing with anxious ones.

Mom found a parking spot near my residence hall. As soon as we stepped out of the car, we were hit by the energy - laughter, doors slamming, someone shouting a greeting down the hall, a stereo playing music somewhere. My residence hall was a tall brick building that looked intimidatingly large to me. A banner over the entrance read "Welcome New Students!" in cheerful letters.

We grabbed as many of my things as we could carry in one trip: I slung a duffel over my shoulder and grabbed two boxes, while Mom took my suitcase and another bag. We followed the stream of other freshmen. In the lobby, a harried-looking resident assistant checked me in, handed me a key and a welcome packet, and gave quick directions to my room on the third floor.

There was an elevator, but it was jam-packed and slow, so Mom and I hauled everything up the stairwell. By the time we reached room 314, we were both a little out of breath. The door was propped open. Inside, my new roommate was already there with his family, unpacking.

He was a lanky guy with sandy brown hair and wire-rimmed glasses. When I appeared in the doorway, he broke into a friendly grin. "Hey! You must be James. I'm Evan."

"Hi, Evan." I manoeuvred in with my boxes and set them down. "Nice to meet you."

His mom and dad nodded at us in greeting. They had clearly been at it for a hile;

Evan's side of the room was half set-up - bed neatly made, a mini-fridge in the corner, a poster of some rock band already taped to the wall.

My side, by contrast, was empty, the bare mattress and desk awaiting my things. I suddenly felt self-conscious about my own belongings - second-hand and simple, next to what looked like brand-new dorm gear that Evan had.

Mom, however, didn't miss a beat. With her characteristic efficiency, she shook hands with Evan's parents and then turned to me, gently taking the box I still held out of my arms. "Let's get you set up, honey."

We spent the next hour organizing my half of the room. Mom made the bed with the sheets she'd washed and packed, while I stacked my books on the shelf above the desk and hooked up the reading lamp. We chatted amiably with Evan and his parents. I learned Evan was from a different state, had two younger sisters, and was majoring in biology. I shared that I was excited (and nervous) to be here and that I hadn't declared a major yet, but was considering English or maybe psychology - I wasn't entirely sure. It felt oddly adult to be having this polite conversation, like we were two young professionals rather than teenagers who would be sharing a tiny dorm room.

In truth, I felt a pang of relief that Evan seemed kind and easy-going. One of my worries had been clashing with a roommate - I'd heard horror stories of roommates who partied all night or stole things. But Evan, with his neat label maker (I noticed he had labelled his desk drawers) and his family's warmth, gave off a reassuring vibe.

At one point, while Mom and I were unrolling my rug (a small striped rug Aunt Nia had gifted me for the dorm), Evan and his dad left to get another load from their car. His mom stayed behind, making small talk with us. She complimented the quilt Mom had packed for my bed - a handmade patchwork quilt that Grandma and Mom had sewn together when I was little, using fabric from some of Mom's old dresses and even some of my baby clothes. I casually mentioned the story behind it.

Evan's mom smiled, touching one of the patches gently. "That's wonderful. It's clear you're very loved."

I glanced at Mom, who was focusing intently on smoothing the rug, her face turned away.
I knew she was hiding tears again. I was grateful to Evan's mom for her kindness, but also felt a protective urge to shorten this conversation before it got too emotional.

Not long after, Evan and his dad returned with the final things, and soon their goodbyes began. His parents gave him quick hugs, reminded him to call, and then gave me friendly waves as they departed. "Take care of each other, you two," Evan's dad said lightly, and then it was just me, Mom, and my new roommate standing in the middle of Room 314.

Evan cleared his throat. "I'm gonna go check out the lounge and meet some of the other guys." He likely sensed my mom and I could use a private goodbye. "Catch you in a bit,

James."

As the door closed behind him, I realized this was it. The moment I'd been both dreading and anticipating all day.

Mom looked around the room one last time, probably checking if there was anything left to do. There wasn't. She had done everything she could to settle me in, just like always.
Now came the time to let go.

I shifted on my feet, not sure what to do with my hands. "Well... I guess that's everything."

She turned to me, and I saw her eyes shining. "Yeah," she said softly. For a second, she simply looked at me, as if trying to memorize my face. I was suddenly very aware that for the first time in my life, I'd be someplace where she wasn't just a room away, or a phone call away (well, she was a phone call away, but it felt different). If something went wrong, if I got sick, if I had a bad day - I'd have to handle it myself first, or lean on new people.

"You're gonna do great here," Mom said, breaking into my thoughts. She reached up to cup my cheek with her palm in a rare gesture of open affection. "I know you'll thrive. Just remember, if you ever feel lost or overwhelmed... you're not alone, okay? You've got people here, and you've got us back home rooting for you."

I nodded, pressing my hand over hers against my face. "I know, Mom." My voice was barely above a whisper.

She opened her arms then, and I hugged her. I hugged her with everything in me, inhaling the familiar scent of her perfume and the faint hint of antiseptic from her nurse's scrubs (which she always seemed to carry with her no matter how much she washed up). She was shaking a little, and I realized I was too.

"Thank you," I managed to choke out. "For everything. I won't let you down."

She pulled back enough to look at me sternly through her tears. "You could never let me down, James. Do you hear me? Never. I'm already so proud of you." She sniffed and tried to smile. "Just be yourself and do your best. That's all I ever ask."

I nodded, unable to speak for the moment. We held each other for a bit longer, and then, with a deep breath, Mom stepped back.

"Okay," she said, wiping her eyes. "I should get on the road before it gets dark." She brushed a stray thread off my shoulder, a final motherly touch that made my chest ache.

I walked her to the car. The campus was golden in the late afternoon light. Many of the other families were gone by now; a new group of students was congregating near the dorm entrance, laughing and trading introductions; the first bonds of friendship forming in real time.

At the car, Mom hesitated with her hand on the open driver's side door. It reminded me of all the times she'd dropped me off somewhere - school, a friend's house - and the little wave she'd give. Only this time she wasn't just driving away for a day.

"I love you, honey," she said softly.

"I love you too, Mom." My voice cracked.

"Call me when you get the chance. Even just to say hi."

"I will. I promise. I'll call you in a couple days, once things settle."

She nodded, then she reached into her pocket. "I almost forgot. Here." She pressed a folded piece of paper into my hand. "Don't read it now. Later tonight, maybe. It's just something I wanted to tell you."

I glanced at the paper, my name written on it in her neat handwriting. My throat constricted. "Okay."

Another hug, one more kiss on my forehead, and then she got into the car. I stepped back onto the curb, hands shoved in my pockets to keep from reaching out to stop her from leaving.

She started the engine, gave me a teary smile through the window, and then the car pulled away. I stayed there watching until the blue sedan turned the corner and disappeared, the same way I had watched Grandpa and Aunt Nia fade from view earlier.

And then, silence. For the first time ever, I was truly on my own.

I stood there for a minute or two, in that silence, feeling the weight of it. The evening air was cooling, filled with the chirp of crickets and the distant sound of laughter from somewhere on campus. I realized I was still clutching the letter Mom had given me.

Back in my dorm room - my dorm room, that still sounded strange - I found that Evan hadn't returned yet. I sat on my bed, the plastic mattress crinkling a little under me, and unfolded the piece of paper with careful hands.

Mom's letter was short and a little smudged, as if she'd been crying while writing it. In it, she told me how proud she was of the young man I had become, how she knew I would do good things in the world. She reminded me to take care of myself, and to remember that it was okay to ask for help when I needed it. The last line read: *You are never alone, my son. Even when we're apart, I am with you and you are with me. Love, Mom.*

I pressed the letter to my face and let the tears come then, quietly in the privacy of that small room. All the emotions of the day - the excitement, the fear, the sadness of saying goodbye - washed over me. I wasn't sure how long I sat there, but by the time I took a deep breath and refolded the letter, I felt a strange calm. Mom was right. Her love, and the love of all those who supported me, wasn't going to vanish just because I was in a new place. I dried my eyes, carefully placed the letter in my desk drawer where I could easily find it later, and inhaled deeply.

This was the beginning of a new chapter - literally Chapter 7 of my story and metaphorically - and I had to step into it.

# Welcome to College

The first week of college was a blur of orientation and a steep learning curve. On my second day, I attempted laundry and overloaded the machine, spending a frantic half hour mopping sudsy water from the basement floor - a lesson in not paying rapt attention to Mom's instructions. Budgeting was another quick reality check; late-night pizza runs and club T-shirts quickly depleted my allowance. I had to remember Mom's constant refrain: *buy what we need first, and there's no shame in saying 'I can't afford that right now.'* I tightened the reins on my spending and learned to prioritize. The biggest challenge was time management. High on the freedom of no parental oversight, I once binged a show until 3 a.m. and paid for it with bleary eyes in my 8 a.m. lecture. Later, panicking over a midterm, I got a FaceTime call from Rico back home. I confessed I'd procrastinated.

"When we'd mess up at the shop, we fix it. So fix it. Go study," he told me. I laughed, hung up, and dove back into my notes. With renewed focus, I managed to pull out a decent grade. Each stumble taught me and forced me to adjust quickly. It wasn't an A, but it was earned honestly with a lot of late-night effort and some energy drinks. There was no Mom or teacher to bail me out if I slacked.

Socially, independence was an adventure. In high school, I had a tight group of friends and a safe routine. In college, I was suddenly surrounded by thousands of peers, each with different backgrounds and expectations. The first few days, I felt like a small fish thrown into an ocean. It seemed like everyone else already knew the deal - where to go, how to act, how to make friends effortlessly. Meanwhile, I walked around campus with a map in my hand (this was before I memorized the shortcuts between buildings) and an awkward half-smile on my face that probably made me look lost (which I was).

Fortunately, people were generally friendly. I met my first new friend in the most random way: I was lugging a huge box of textbooks back from the bookstore, and a tall guy with dreadlocks came jogging up. "You need a hand with that, man?" he asked.

His name was Marcus - not the Marcus from middle school who had fought me, but a tall, lanky sophomore who coincidentally shared the same first name. I smiled at the cosmic irony of that. This Marcus was majoring in Computer Science and lived on the floor below mine. He helped carry half my books and we got to talking. By the time we reached my dorm, we'd exchanged numbers and he invited me to join a pick-up basketball game that weekend.

That invite felt like a lifeline. Stepping onto the campus rec center court that Saturday with Marcus and a bunch of guys I'd never met, I was nervous I wouldn't measure up. Despite all the basketball I had played in high school, I didn't really consider myself a star. Some of them were really good - clearly high school varsity players, maybe one or two who could've been playing for our college team but chose intramurals instead.

What struck me, though, was how I immediately tried to gauge the kind of masculinity that ruled here. Was this going to be the chest-thumping, trash-talking scene I'd tried to survive in my younger days? My mind flashed to Darius, the particularly brash teammate from high school who dominated the locker room with his aggressive energy. But here on this court, things were surprisingly chill. Yes, there was competition - a few guys yelled out jibes when someone missed a shot, and there was plenty of laughter and high-fives - but it didn't feel toxic. It felt fun.

I even heard one guy, Sam, apologize good-naturedly when he accidentally elbowed another during a rebound. That simple "My bad, you good?" followed by a pat on the back was a small revelation: you could be strong and competitive and still courteous. *Strength and tenderness*, as Mom might frame it - not that these guys would call it that, but that's what it was in action.

Playing that day loosened something in me. We played hard for two hours, and by the end, sweaty and exhausted, I realized I'd not only had a great time, I'd also earned a bit of respect from them simply by playing fair and not giving up when it got intense. My team lost more games than we won, but I hit a couple of nice shots and hustled on defence. That was enough. Marcus clapped me on the back when we finished, "Yo, James, we're grabbing burgers, you down?"

Sitting in a booth at a burger joint just off campus, surrounded by the easy banter of these new friends, I felt something I hadn't since arriving - a sense of belonging. We talked about majors, laughed about our disastrous attempts at cooking in the dorm (one guy set off the fire alarm making popcorn), and yes, there was some classic guy humour and talk about girls and which dorms had the cutest ones - but it wasn't mean-spirited. It felt, dare I say, wholesome, or at least normal and light.

One thing I did notice: a couple of the guys started lightly ribbing one of our group, a quiet freshman named Jon, about not drinking. "Man, we gotta get you to a party. Loosen you up!" they joked. Jon turned red and mumbled something about focusing on studies. They didn't push too hard, but I saw that flash of discomfort. It reminded me of times I felt pressured to be someone I wasn't.

Later that evening, as I walked back to my dorm, I got to chatting with Jon. He admitted he was a bit nervous about the party scene - his father had struggled with alcoholism, so he was determined to stay away from it. I told him about my own wariness of certain scenes, how in high school I often felt like an outsider to the "macho" party culture. We bonded over that. It felt good to be honest, and I realized something important - *I wasn't the only one*. Everyone had their own stories, their own worries. As Mom always says, "everyone has a story," and here I was hearing them firsthand from new people.

In those first months, new male figures started appearing in my life. They weren't replacing the mentors I had back home; rather, they were adding to my understanding of what manhood could look like.

Take my roommate, Evan - he surprised me. With his neatly labelled belongings and disciplined study habits, he showed me a version of young manhood that was thoughtful and organized. He often talked to his girlfriend back home in the evenings, his voice gentle, and he wasn't shy about saying "I love you" to her on the phone even with me in the room. That openness with his feelings struck me. We had late-night conversations about our families, and he told me his dad was a stay-at-home dad when he was younger while his mom worked, which was something I'd never encountered. "So my dad cooks better than my mom," he joked once, but I could tell he was proud of both his parents.

Evan was a mirror of a different sort - reflecting qualities like responsibility and emotional openness that I respected.

Then there was Professor Shannon, my English 101 instructor. A tall Black man in his fifties, with salt-and-pepper hair and a voice that somehow managed to be both gentle and commanding. On the first day of class, he recited a Langston Hughes poem from memory and talked about the power of owning your story. I felt like he was speaking directly to me. Encouraged by Mr. Thompson's parting gift and note, I had dared to register for an intro to creative writing course as an elective, which Prof. Shannon taught.

One afternoon, I hung back after class and introduced myself properly. "Professor, I really enjoyed that essay you assigned," I said, referring to a piece we'd read about identity and heritage.

He looked up from gathering his papers and gave me a warm smile. "Thank you... James, right?" I was pleasantly surprised he knew my name already.

"Yes, sir," I said, then felt slightly silly for the 'sir' (we were usually on first-name basis in college, but some habits die hard). I added, "I actually wanted to ask - do you have any suggestions for improving my writing? I... I like to write, but I've never shared much of it."

Professor Shannon set his satchel down and gestured for me to sit. We ended up talking for fifteen minutes. He asked me what I liked to write about. Hesitantly, I told him I'd kept journals growing up, and that I sometimes wrote about my family. He nodded as if this were the most natural thing. "Writing can be a powerful way to understand ourselves," he said. "If you ever want to share something, I'd be happy to read it. And have you considered joining the campus literary magazine? They're always looking for new voices."

I remembered Mr. Thompson and the writing club in high school, how it took me until junior year to join because I was shy. Here was a chance to start fresh, to define myself anew. "I... I'll think about it," I replied.

Professor Shannon then told me something that stayed with me:

*James, your perspective – who you are, where you come from – that is your strength. Don't shy away from it. A lot of young men think they have to wear a mask or fit a mould. But trust me, the most compelling stories, the most compelling people, are those who know themselves and stay true to that.*

As I left his office, I realized I had just met another mentor. He wasn't replacing Mr. Thompson or Coach or anyone else; he was another guide, offering me wisdom at the next stage of my journey.

## Shadows on Campus

Still, not all influences around me were positive. There were shadows, you could say, lurking in the periphery of campus life. One particularly loud one was a junior named Andre who lived on our floor. Andre projected an aura of toughness and bravado that reminded me a bit of the bullies and "cool kids" from back home. He blared hip-hop music at all hours, boasted loudly about his exploits with girls, and had an entourage of impressionable freshmen who hung on his every word. He wasn't in any of my classes, but you could feel Andre holding court in the common room or by the dorm entrance, regaling others with stories of how he cheated on a test and never got caught, or how he could drink any under the table.

At first, I'll admit, I was a little drawn to that confidence. It was like seeing the

embodiment of what teenage me thought a "real man" was supposed to be - carefree, assertive, getting what he wants without apology. Andre even tried to buddy up with me a couple of times when he learned I played basketball. We shot hoops behind the dorm now and then, and he'd give me advice that was less about technique and more about attitude:

"You gotta show 'em you're the alpha, James. On the court, in class, with the ladies - it's all the same game. Don't ever show weakness."

I recognized the rhetoric. It was the shadow side of all the positive lessons I'd learned. The idea that manhood was a game of domination, where vulnerability was a flaw. In a strange way, I was glad to encounter Andre, because he forced me to consciously choose what kind of man I wanted to be. He was like a shadow cast on the wall - a shape of manhood that was hollow in some ways. Sure, he was charismatic and not entirely a bad guy; occasionally, I saw glimpses of genuine kindness in him, like when he lent one of the freshmen his textbook for a class they shared. But then he'd mask it with a flippant remark, like he couldn't let anyone think he was actually caring.

One night, a bunch of us were hanging in the dorm lounge watching a late-night talk show. The host had a guest on who was a famous male actor, talking about his struggles with depression and how therapy helped him. I found it insightful, but Andre scoffed. "This guy's soft," he said loudly. "Airin' out his feelings on TV. Man, back in the day, dudes just dealt with their problems. All this crying to therapists... that's weak."

A few people chuckled or nodded, but I couldn't stay silent. My heart was thudding in my chest because challenging someone like Andre in front of others took guts, and the ghost of middle-school me was anxious about it. But I thought of Mom, of Mr. Thompson's counsel that vulnerability can be strength.

"That's not weak," I said, trying to keep my tone calm. "Talking about that stuff... it takes a lot of guts actually."

Andre gave me a look - half surprised, half dismissive. "You sayin' you'd go cry to a shrink, James?"

"I'm saying," I replied, my voice steadying, "that everyone has problems. Not everyone faces them. Admitting you need help or that you're hurting... I think that's pretty strong.
Cowards hide stuff, right?"

The lounge got quiet. Andre stared at me, and I could see the gears turning in his head.
This was a public challenge, albeit a polite one. Part of me braced for him to make me a target of ridicule.

But something interesting happened. One of the freshmen who idolized him piped up, "I dunno, Dre. My uncle's in therapy, and he's like the toughest dude I know. PTSD from the army. He says it helps."

Andre snorted, but didn't have a comeback. The attention of the room shifted away as the show moved on to a comedy segment. Later, as we all filtered out of the lounge, Andre lingered. As I walked past him, he said quietly, "You one of those sensitive guys, huh?" It wasn't said kindly, but oddly, it didn't feel like a full insult either.

I paused, meeting his eyes. "Just not afraid to be human," I said.

He nodded ever so slightly - a gesture I might have missed if I wasn't looking for it - and then we went our separate ways. We weren't going to be close friends, Andre and I, but I realized I didn't want to be a shadow like him, defined by bluster and afraid of my own soft spots.

# The Manhood Equation

One crisp evening in late October, I took a walk alone across campus. The quad was ablaze with red and gold leaves, a few students throwing a frisbee in the cooling air. I had just left a study session at the library. My mind was buzzing with thoughts - an upcoming paper, a meeting and an email from Coach Simmons I'd received saying he heard from Mom that I was doing well and to keep it up. Coach wasn't one for long emails, but just seeing his short note felt like a hug from home. All those voices of support from my past were still with me, but now I was mixing them with new voices.

As I walked, I thought about something Professor Shannon had said in class that week, quoting a writer: *"You have to define yourself, or others will define you."* It resonated deeply. I had spent my early teens letting others define what manhood should look like and feeling I came up short. By the end of high school, I started carving out my own definition, thanks to mentors and hard-won lessons. Now, away from home, that process was truly mine. I could fall into patterns of trying to please others, to be what I thought they expected, or I could be myself, even if that self was still a work in progress.

That was when I made a quiet promise to myself: I would define manhood on my own terms. For me, it wouldn't be measured by bluster or stoicism, but by **Integrity** - doing the right thing even when it was hard; **Responsibility** - taking ownership for my actions and fixing what I broke; and **Self-knowledge** - the courage to know what I valued, what I felt, and not being afraid of any of it. I realized my own blueprint was becoming solid.

Later that night, I ended up calling Mom, past her bedtime. When she picked up, I told her, "I'm okay, nothing's wrong. I just... wanted to say hi." She relaxed and laughed.

Before hanging up, I said, "You know, I've been thinking. You and everyone back home gave me such a strong foundation. I'm really grateful." Her voice got that tender, warm tone. "We just helped you find what was already in you, baby. And I am so proud of the man you're becoming."

I lay in bed in the dark, and realized I was finally truly becoming myself - the man I wanted to be, not the one I thought I had to be.

# CHAPTER 8

# THE LOVE, INTIMACY & RELATIONSHIPS OF A MAN

The manhood complex would always get worse when relationships came into the picture. Amid the throng of students at a crowded freshman mixer, I caught sight of a girl dancing goofily with her friends. She had deep brown skin, a halo of curly hair, and an uninhibited joy that immediately drew me. Evan nudged me to go talk to her.

My stomach did a little flip; in high school, I'd been shy, but her genuine laughter emboldened me. I edged closer, and just as the song changed, our eyes met.

I felt heat rush to my face, but I managed a smile.

"I like your moves," I shouted over the music. "I'm James."

She grinned, a little breathless. "Imani." That was how I met my first woman.

## Imani

I quickly motioned toward the lobby. "How about some punch? I could use a break." Relief washed over me. We talked haltingly at first, then more easily. I learned she was a freshman studying sociology, and I came away more smitten with every word. I was always cautious, ensuring I showed deep respect for her boundaries—a quality instilled by Mom. I'd offer to walk her to her dorm, but I'd stop short of any gesture that felt too forward.

A few weeks into our friendship, we went to an outdoor movie night on campus. We sat on the lawn, and as the night air grew chilly, I draped the blanket more around her. She gave me a grateful smile and snuggled closer. My palms were sweating, but I decided to go for it. I reached out and let my hand rest lightly on the back of hers. She turned her hand over so our palms touched, interlacing her fingers with mine. I barely paid attention to the rest of the movie. After the credits rolled, we walked to her dorm, where she gave me a quick peck on the cheek. My cheek tingled; my first foray into romance was a series of small, tender moments, and I liked that a lot.

Imani and I started dating "officially" after that night. Neither of us made a big announcement or anything, but soon it was understood that when we went to meals or events, we were going as a pair. I'd hold her hand as we strolled through campus, and the nervousness I initially felt gave way to an easy joy. Being with her felt comfortable and exciting at once.

In this first serious relationship of my life, I discovered ways that being raised by a woman had quietly prepared me.

For one, communication. Mom always valued talking things through - even if teenage me sometimes resisted - and with Imani I found it relatively natural to listen and to share.

When she had a bad day because of a tough exam or a spat with her roommate, I found myself doing what Mom often did with me: listening attentively, offering empathy first rather than immediate advice. Imani once joked, "You're such a good listener. Are you sure you're real?" which made me laugh but also made me a bit proud. If there was one thing I wanted to excel at as a boyfriend, it was to not be the oblivious or self-centred guy stereotype.

I also noticed I had a deep reservoir of respect that guided how I treated her. For example, I always walked her to her dorm at night, not because I thought she couldn't handle herself, but because Mom had instilled in me the importance of ensuring those you care about feel safe. Imani told me she appreciated that I never assumed things - like if she said she was too busy to hang out, I never guilted her or got upset; I'd just say "I understand" and mean it. I think watching Mom handle so much alone made me conscious of not adding stress to anyone's life, especially someone I cared for.

Those were our strengths: empathy, respect, patience. But there were challenges, too. One early challenge came in the form of my own guardedness. Despite being generally communicative, I realized I had a habit of holding back on expressing my deeper insecurities or needs. Part of it was not wanting to burden anyone - a mentality I got from seeing how much Mom carried; I didn't want to add to someone else's load with my issues.

Another part was that I'd never really had to articulate these tender spots to anyone outside my family.

I recall one evening in late winter, Imani and I were studying in the library. I was unusually quiet and tense, worried about Grandpa's health issues and my cut work-study hours. Instead of telling Imani, I retreated into myself, forcing a smile when she asked if I was okay. I just cited "classes" as the problem, sensing her subtle disappointment. Later, in a quiet moment in my dorm, Imani gently broached it. "You don't always let me be there for you," she said softly. "You don't have to protect me from everything."

Her words made my chest tighten. I realized I was pushing her away out of habit, trying to shield her from my burdens just as Mom had shielded me. I squeezed her hand and mustered the courage to share: I told her about Grandpa and the financial stress. The more I talked, the easier it got. She listened just as I would for her, then gave me a hug and simply said, "Thank you for telling me." It felt like a balm to my soul. All those lessons from Mom about strength and tenderness clicked into place—this was a space where I could be tender, and it wouldn't make me weak or less of a man.

All those lessons from Mom about strength and tenderness clicked into place differently - this was a space where I could be tender, and it wouldn't make me weak or less of a man in her eyes.

Still, growth is rarely linear.

Over the next year and a half, Imani and I grew very close. We navigated the typical college couple things: coordinating time together amid busy schedules, supporting each other through exam stress, even spending part of holidays apart and missing one another (I sent her corny selfies to cheer her up when we were each at our respective homes over winter break). She met Mom when she came to visit me one weekend; I was a bit nervous, but Mom was her warm self and later told me privately, "She's lovely. And I can tell she cares about you." Imani later admitted she'd been nervous to meet my mother - "I wanted her to like me. Your mom is kind of your hero, you know." That was the moment I realized how obvious my reverence for Mom was, and it made me both proud and a little concerned. Proud because yes, Mom is my hero. Concerned because I wondered if that put pressure on Imani, or any girl I dated - like they were silently competing with this ideal I held of my mother. There you have it; the worst-case scenarios slowly begin to creep in.

Truth be told, I did sometimes compare. Not consciously in a "you're not like my mom" way - but I had an ingrained expectation of how a woman should carry herself: with strength and kindness, because that's what I saw growing up. It's unfair to put anyone on a pedestal like that, and I caught myself whenever I noticed it. Imani, to her credit, was her own woman, different from Mom in many ways. Mom's a neat freak, Imani was notoriously messy with clothes strewn everywhere; Mom is an early riser, Imani studied best after midnight. And that was okay. I loved those differences as much as the similarities.

Our first big rough patch came in spring of sophomore year. Imani had the chance to study abroad in France for a semester. It was a dream opportunity for her, and I was excited on her behalf, but as the time for her departure neared, I grew anxious about doing long-distance. We promised to stay in touch, and we did - at first. But the six-hour time difference and both of our packed schedules (her immersed in travel and new experiences, me knee-deep in a particularly tough course load and a new role as a peer tutor on campus) made it challenging. Our calls turned into brief texts. There was no blow-up, no betrayal but just this slow drifting that neither of us knew how to stop.

One night, after a missed Skype date that we'd planned (she forgot, I fell asleep waiting - it was a mess of bad timing), I wrote in my journal: *"Is this how things end? Not with a bang but with a whimper?"* I was heartsick and also frustrated with myself. I worried that maybe I wasn't fighting hard enough to keep the connection strong. But a part of me also wondered if this was a natural fork in the road. We were nineteen, with paths temporarily diverging.

When she returned in the fall of our junior year, we tried to rekindle what we had. We had a sweet reunion at the airport, holding each other tightly. For a while, it felt like old times, though I noticed she had changed in subtle ways: there was a new confidence in her stride, a broadened perspective from living abroad. I admired it, but I also felt a tad insecure.
Had I grown in the time apart? Or was I standing still?

We gave it an honest try for a couple more months. Ultimately, it was an evening in November, sitting on a bench under the leafless oak trees on campus, that we had "the talk."

"I feel like we're out of sync," she said gently, her hands in mine, both of us bundled in coats. There were tears in her eyes. I'm sure there were in mine too.

"I know," I exhaled. "It's like we're trying to go back to how it was, but we're not those people anymore, are we?"

She shook her head, a tear rolling down her cheek. I caught it with my thumb, an instinctive affectionate gesture that made us both cry a little more.

"I love you, James," she said. "You were my first... everything. I will always care about you."

"I love you too, Imani." My voice broke. "So much."

We sat in silence, holding each other. The idea of actually saying the words "let's break up" felt too painful to utter, but in that silence we both knew. We had given each other so much, but our paths were diverging. She had big plans, talking about applying for internships in New York, possibly grad school abroad. I, too, was thinking ahead, considering an internship in another state that coming summer. We were growing up and, as much as it hurt, perhaps growing apart.

The breakup, when it became official, was as gentle as a heartbreak could be. There was just a deep sadness and mutual respect. We parted with another hug, and then I watched her walk away across the quad, wiping her eyes. It felt like each step she took was away from our chapter together.

In the weeks that followed, I experienced heartbreak for the first time. Real heartbreak - the kind that sits in your chest like a stone and makes the world look a little greyer. I threw myself into activities, I doubled down on studying, hit the gym more, joined a volunteer committee, anything to keep busy so I wouldn't dwell on the emptiness where her daily presence used to be.

Of course, I had to process it. One night, a couple of weeks after the breakup, I found myself parked in my car outside a late-night donut shop off campus. The radio was playing a song that Imani loved, and that's when the tears came—big, heaving sobs that took me by surprise. If there was any moment I felt the absence of a father in my life, it was then; I didn't know how men were "supposed" to handle heartbreak. Instead of calling Mom and worrying her, I dialed Aunt Nia.

"We broke up... and I don't know what to do... It hurts," I choked out. She listened for a good hour, occasionally offering words of comfort. "It's okay to hurt. It means it was real," she soothed. "The fact that you treat women with respect and care, that's not a flaw, that's a strength. You'll take what you learned from this and do even better next time."

Her words were a balm, reminding me not to close my big heart. I promised I would try.

Over the next few months, I did heal, bit by bit. I focused on myself - something I'd heard people say after breakups and discovered to be true. I poured more energy into the campus literary magazine that I had finally joined, thanks to Professor Shannon's encouragement. Writing became a solace; I even wrote a piece about heartbreak that got published in the magazine. It was raw and honest. I wrote about the quiet of my dorm room after Imani stopped coming by, and about the way I had folded the blanket we used at the outdoor movie and put it away out of sight. Writing it out felt cathartic, and a couple of readers - including a girl in my class - told me it resonated with them. That made me feel less alone.

I also grew closer to some friends during that time, especially a woman named Tara, a fellow editor on the lit magazine.

## Tara

Tara was funny, outspoken, and a great writer. We spent many late nights in the publication office, arranging layouts and choosing submissions. She had a boyfriend at another college, so it was purely platonic between us, which oddly allowed me to relax and just be myself. Through our friendship, I saw another facet of male-female relationships: not every connection had to be romantic or lead somewhere. We could just be friends who supported each other. When I mentioned offhand that I'd gone through a breakup, she showed up next meeting with homemade cookies "to mend a broken heart," she said with a grin. It was a small gesture, but it warmed me.

In turn, when she had a fight with her distant boyfriend, I listened, gave some perspective, and even told her one of Mom's lines: *"everyone has a story."* It was a reminder to her that maybe her boyfriend's outburst wasn't about her but something he was dealing with.
She later told me that helped her approach the situation with more empathy, and they patched things up. It felt good to exchange that kind of support without any ulterior motives or complications. It reinforced what Mom had taught me by example: women are people to value and learn from, not puzzles to solve or prizes to win. Having Tara as a friend made that truth even clearer.

By senior year, I felt like a more mature, though slightly scarred, version of myself. I had loved deeply and lost, and I survived. More than that, I grew. I reflected often on what went right and wrong with Imani. One critical lesson I learned was that love requires vulnerability from both people - and sometimes, even with love, two people grow in different directions. And that's okay. It doesn't mean the time together was a failure.

Another lesson was about communication. With Imani, we'd been pretty good at it, but during the study abroad separation, we both hesitated to voice our fears (fear of drifting, fear of holding each other back). I promised myself I wouldn't let fear of an uncomfortable conversation lead to a slow fading again. Better to be upfront, even if it hurts, than to lose something by default.

Little did I know I'd get to put that to the test soon.

In the spring of my senior year, a new chapter of romance began almost when I least expected it. I was busy with final projects and job applications, not actively looking for anything. Then I met Alisha.

# Alisha

I met Alisha in a community service club; she was a junior, a transfer student with a magnetic smile and a calm presence. Over planning sessions for a local reading program, we clicked. I missed talking to her when the project ended, so coffee led to dinner, which led to a weekend hike. When Alisha and I talked, I found myself being more open from the get-go. She also grew up with a single mom, which gave us an instant, quiet understanding. I realized I was being given an opportunity to apply what I'd learned: to engage in this budding relationship with more honesty from the start. I even told her about my past relationship, and she listened thoughtfully, offering a non-judgmental response that made me feel safe.

So, when I felt we were ready to define whatever was building between us, I was the one who brought it up (something I might have been too timid to do a couple years earlier). We were in the student union after a club meeting, lingering at a table as the building cleared out.

"Alisha," I said, heart thumping, "I really enjoy spending time with you. More than that, actually. I think you're amazing."

She looked up from stirring the remnants of her tea, studying my face with those warm brown eyes of hers. A slow smile formed. "I really enjoy spending time with you too, James."

I exhaled a breath I hadn't realized I was holding. "Would you... maybe like to make this official? Like, be my girlfriend?" It sounded old-fashioned even as I said it, but I wanted clarity for both of us.

She laughed softly. "I was wondering when you'd ask. Yes, I would like that."

And just like that, I had a girlfriend again, and this time I felt like I stepped into it with eyes wide open and lessons in mind.

From the very beginning, I approached things differently. I made conscious efforts to be transparent about my feelings and to encourage her to do the same. For instance, early on I told her about my occasional anxiety with finances and future plans, because it was on my mind as graduation neared. I admitted I sometimes overthink things. She, in turn, shared that she had moments of insecurity, especially having transferred schools and still finding her place. We created a safe space, often just by saying, "I feel…" or "I need…," phrases that sound simple but can be so hard to say for fear of sounding needy or weak.
Yet what we found was that by voicing those things, we actually grew closer and built trust.

A challenge arose a couple of months in, which became a chance to prove growth. I had applied for a job in another state—a good entry-level opportunity. The old James might have downplayed this to avoid a tough conversation, but with Alisha, that didn't feel right.
I told her honestly about the job and that I had a good chance at it. "Thank you for telling me," she said, her voice sincere. "Most guys I dated would have just waited until plans were set and said 'oh by the way…' But you didn't." I felt relieved that this hadn't devolved into drama.

Ultimately, I did get that job offer, and we faced the prospect of distance. We discussed it openly; she still had a year of school, and I didn't want to give up a good job opportunity.
The night we decided this, I called Mom. She trusted me to make the right choice but offered one piece of advice:

*Love isn't always convenient, honey. If it's worth*
*it, you'll find a way. And if it's not, you'll know.*
*But don't let fear be the only reason you stop or go.*
*Make the choice from love or not at all.*

Alisha and I chose to keep our love, deciding to try long-distance with clear agreements: honesty, regular visits, and a mutual understanding that we would openly discuss it if it became too hard. We chose based on what we truly felt and wanted, not just what we were scared of.

Alisha and I chose to keep our love, even if it meant some struggle.

This relationship felt different in its maturity. There was passion and affection, yes, but also a steady companionship, a partnership of two people who respected each other's individual journey as much as the journey together. We celebrated each other's wins, like when she got an important summer internship or when I aced my senior thesis presentation. We also made space for each other's friends; I became good friends with her circle and she with mine. There wasn't that insular "just us" bubble that sometimes first loves can have. We were integrated into each other's lives more fully.

As I approached graduation, I reflected on how being raised by Mom had prepared me for this facet of life. Watching her navigate relationships (or often, her choice to focus on raising me without dating much) taught me to value commitment and not to take lightly the decision to invite someone into your life. She used to say, "Don't ever be with someone who makes you less you. The right person will make you more you." I finally understood that. With Alisha, I felt like more me - the best version, even as I continued to grow. And I hoped I did the same for her.

I also recognized how Mom's lessons on empathy were a gift in love. When Alisha and I had disagreements - and we did have a few, like when she felt I wasn't making enough time for her during a busy period, or when I felt a twinge of jealousy about one of her male friends (I admitted it, we talked it through) - in those moments, trying to see the situation through her eyes made all the difference. Instead of reacting defensively, I tried to really hear what she was saying and feeling, and she did the same for me. It's not that we were perfect; one time I snapped at her when I was stressed, and I immediately felt awful. I showed up at her door an hour later with takeout from her favourite Chinese place and an apology at the ready. She smiled and said, "I know you didn't mean it. Thank you for saying sorry." In those simple exchanges, I realized being "raised by a woman" gave me a leg up in understanding that apologizing isn't weakness, and that caring gestures go a long way to heal small wounds.

On the flip side, I also had to learn to assert myself when needed - something that maybe I wasn't as good at initially. For example, in my first relationship, I might have been too accommodating at times, afraid to upset my girlfriend by saying no to things or by expressing when something bothered me. With Alisha, I was more confident to speak up.
Once, when I felt she jokingly belittled one of my hobbies in front of friends, I told her later that it actually hurt my feelings. She was mortified that she'd hurt me and apologized. But that was a growth point for me: to not just swallow hurt out of fear of conflict. I suspect having mentors like Coach and Mr. Thompson, and generally feeling more secure in myself by this age, helped with that too.

As senior year drew to a close, I found myself truly appreciating how love and intimacy had shaped me - and how my upbringing had shaped my approach to them. On the eve of graduation, I sat in my dorm (mostly packed up by then) and wrote in my journal. I wrote a letter of sorts to Mom (though I didn't give it to her; it was more for me). In it, I reflected on how her love taught me to love others: with kindness, patience, and honesty. I wrote about how seeing her strength and independence taught me to value those traits in my partners, but also how her unwavering support showed me it's okay to lean on someone you love.

I thought about something else too: how being raised by a single mother had, in a way, shown me the kind of man I didn't want to be. My father's absence was like an inverse lesson. I didn't want to be someone who walked away, who left responsibilities behind. I wanted to be present, reliable, the kind of man who would stay through the hard conversations and the tough times. Of course, I had no idea what my father's story truly was (perhaps he had his own pains and reasons), but from my perspective, he abandoned a woman and child who loved him. I never wanted to inflict that kind of absence on anyone I loved. I recognized that this might have made me cautious to a fault, but ultimately it also made me conscientious.

By the time I finished writing, I realized that love - whether it was first love, friendship, or a new deeper love - had a way of both exposing my vulnerabilities and fortifying my strengths. And being raised by Mom meant I entered each of those experiences with a heart that was unafraid to be gentle. In a world that sometimes seemed to encourage men to be hard, distant, or flippant about matters of the heart, I wore my heart differently. Yes, it meant I felt the stings deeply, but it also meant I experienced the beauty of intimacy fully.

On graduation day, as I lined up in my cap and gown, I spotted Mom, as always, and Alisha in the crowd of friends attending the ceremony, cheering and snapping pictures. I waved, feeling a swell of gratitude. My journey through love and relationships had not been the stereotypical college playboy story, nor had it been smooth sailing all the way.

But it was mine, true to who I was and who I was raised to be.

# CHAPTER 9

# STRENGHT IN GRATITUDE-
# FINAL MEDITATIONS

By the time my college life was over, I could boldly say I was a fully moulded man, irrespective of what the world and the society thought. I was in my early twenties and the circumstances around me were more than enough to point out the reality that something in me had changed.

The entire world just came in a different view.

## Graduation Ceremony

I can still remember that very day of graduation. As the procession music began and we filed toward our seats, I craned my neck to search the crowd. I knew exactly who I was looking for. And then I spotted her: Mom, seated near the front, thanks to an early arrival, I'm sure. She had on a lovely floral dress I'd never seen before (likely something she bought just for today) and a wide-brimmed sun hat to shield against the June sun. Even from a distance, I could see the unmistakable shimmer of tears on her face, though she was smiling ear to ear. I could also spot Aunt Nia, who was already waving exuberantly in my direction the moment she saw me glance over. It had been about eight months since I last saw them and I had to admit that their faces had changed a whole lot. There was also my girlfriend Alisha a few seats down from them, camcorder in hand as she insisted on filming parts of the ceremony for Mom so she could simply soak in the moment. She had some other friends with her and among the crowd, I could spot some of the juniors with whom I was well acquainted. Seeing all these faces - my people - in one place nearly took my breath away and within me, I felt that surge of emotions of gratitude, pride, and that bittersweet awareness of time's flow.

But it also brought back a lot of memories; significant people that were once present but no more. Grandpa was not present, not after he had passed shortly after Grandma months ago; literally the last thing that brought Mom and I together was the celebration of his funeral. And even as I reminisced over the dear old man, others like Coach Simmons, Mr. Thompson and Mr. Jenkins came to mind; significant chapters of my life that made me who I am presently. Everyone was now pursuing their life somewhere else.

The ceremony itself was both a blur and a collection of vivid snapshots in my memory. The university president gave a speech about the "journey ahead." A student speaker joked about late-night study sessions and the friendships forged. I listened, but my mind drifted, reflecting on my own journey to this point.

Four years ago, I sat in a similar chair at my high school graduation, feeling on the cusp of the unknown, with Mom cheering me on from the stands. In that moment, I'd been painfully aware of my father's absence and simultaneously overwhelmed by the presence of those who stepped in. Now, here I was again, another milestone, and that familiar ache and warmth danced in tandem in my chest but not with the same crushing intensity with which it came when I was much younger.

*Because now, I was my own man.*

After the ceremony concluded, there was a happy chaos of people meeting up with their graduates on the lawn. I wove through the throngs of hugging families until I spotted Mom and the rest coming toward me. Mom reached me first and threw her arms around me, mortarboard hat and all.

"Oh, my baby, I am so proud of you," she cried, voice muffled a bit as she pressed her face to my shoulder. I held her tightly. This small woman, who somehow contained the strength of an army in her, was shaking with sobs of happiness.

"We did it, Mom," I whispered, echoing the words from high school but with even more meaning now. "Thank you. For everything."

She pulled back, cupping my face with both hands. Her eyes were red, makeup slightly smudged at the corners from tears, but I thought she never looked more beautiful. "You earned this, James. You have become such an incredible man. Your dad - " she hesitated, and then continued softly, "Your dad would be proud. And I know he's proud of me too, for raising you." It was one of the rare times she openly mentioned Dad in a positive light.

My eyes stung, and I nodded, placing my hand over hers on my cheek.

Aunt Nia practically danced in to squeeze me next. "You did it, sweet boy!" she exclaimed. "And with honors, don't think I didn't see that cord on your gown!" She stepped back and fanned her face dramatically. "I promised myself I wouldn't cry, but look at me."

I laughed, feeling a warm fullness in my chest at being surrounded by their love. There was a round of congratulations from others - Alisha came up and, after hugging me, politely hugged my mom too. Rico, my childhood friend, was also there; he had driven up with his fiancée to see me graduate. We clasped hands and did a one-armed guy hug.

"Proud of you, man," he said

Eventually, the celebrations wound down. I held Mom tightly, whispering, "We did it, Mom," and she, with tears tracing her cheeks, responded, "You have become such an incredible man. Your dad would be proud." After a round of congratulations from Aunt Nia, Alisha, and Rico, we celebrated with lunch. That summer flew by quickly; Mom insisted on a cookout party before I packed up.

The move to my new job, six hours from home with a nonprofit organization focused on educational outreach, was another significant goodbye. This time, I noticed a different look in Mom's eyes that held less anxiety and more pure pride. As I drove away, I felt emotional, yes, but also ready. Now real life beckoned, and thanks to my upbringing and education, I felt prepared to face it.

*But life was designed to stun you at every stage.*

## The Start of a Profession

My first day at the job, I wore the only suit I owned (the same one I'd used for senior presentations). I stepped into the office which was a medium-sized nonprofit's headquarters, having butterflies in my stomach. The atmosphere was different from any classroom or campus office I'd known. Here, people weren't running on semesters; they were in the thick of year-round projects, real grants, real stakes in communities.

I was introduced to my team that comprised of seasoned staff and a couple of other new hires around my age. My direct supervisor was Mr. Paul Warren, a man in his late fifties and a reputation, I'd soon learn, for being tough as nails. During the brief introduction, he gave me a once-over and a polite nod but was straight to business, "We're glad to have you, James. Hope you're ready to dive in, we have a lot going on." His tone was not unkind, but brisk and no-nonsense.

In the first weeks, I found myself working longer hours than I anticipated, trying to absorb everything. The organization was in the midst of preparing for a big fall initiative - an after-school program launch in several schools - and I, as the newbie program coordinator, was given a stack of tasks from researching educational materials to assisting senior coordinators with logistics.

I quickly learned that the working world expected initiative. In school, you're given a syllabus and clear deadlines. Here, it was more like "here's a broad goal, now figure out how to help achieve it." At first, I was a bit lost, not wanting to make mistakes. I doublechecked everything and asked perhaps too many questions. Mr. Warren, though stern, was willing to answer a few but then expected me to figure things out. "Use your judgment," he would say.

One afternoon, I was tasked with drafting a proposal document for a potential sponsor partnership. I worked diligently on it, checking it against previous documents. When I handed it to Mr. Warren for review, he scanned it and pointed out a few errors like a typo here, a formatting issue there, and an important section I'd left vague.

"Tighten this up," he said curtly, "and next time, double-check before you bring it to me."

His words stung a bit. I wasn't used to such blunt critique. In college, professors usually sandwiched criticism with praise. Here, praise was scarce. You mostly heard about what to fix. I took a breath, swallowed my pride, and nodded.

"I will. Thank you." I stayed late that day making sure every correction was made, triplechecking my work.

As I left the office, the janitor nodded to me kindly - I was one of the last people there besides him. On the drive back to my new apartment, I felt a little deflated. Part of me feared I wasn't cut out for this fast-paced, demanding environment. And then, I went, "Oh, well! Everybody has a bad day. What matters is how you fix it."

Remember, there were no shortcuts - *if you do it, do it right*. Mr. Warren's critique, while brusque, was pushing me to a higher standard. He wanted it done right. And so did I.

The next opportunity I got to prove myself came soon during a community meeting. When one of our speakers was late, Mr. Warren pulled me aside. "We need someone to give a brief overview to kick things off. You up for it?" Though my heart galloped, I stepped up to the podium and spoke from the heart about the mission. Later, Mr. Warren approached me and said, "Good work tonight. You stepped up." I realized that respect in the working world wasn't earned through status, but by showing up, fixing your mistakes, and stepping up when needed. My resilience, a gentle but fierce trait I learned from Mom, showed externally. I tried to treat everyone with the same respect—from the executive director to the janitor. As months went by, I settled into a rewarding rhythm.

Alisha and I kept our relationship going across the distance, visiting every month. We addressed challenges directly, leaning on our foundation of honest communication. I also made friends and, through our program, began mentoring a high school junior named Devin. I found myself echoing Mom's wisdom to him, and when he got a scholarship, I felt immense pride. I began sending a little money home each month. Not that Mom asked—she never would—but I knew a bit of extra could give her breathing room. The first time I insisted on paying a utility bill, she was conflicted, but I replied, "I know, Mom. But let me do this. I want to." This was part of why I worked hard: to give back.

That year, Mother's Day and Father's Day were particularly poignant. For Mother's Day, I sent Mom a full handwritten letter expressing my gratitude for each sacrifice and lesson. She said it was the most meaningful gift she'd ever received. On Father's Day, I called her to wish her "Happy Father's Day," a tradition that, when overheard by a colleague, opened up a conversation about co-parenting struggles, where my simple gesture gave him a new perspective.

By the end of that first year, I had grown in confidence. I felt compelled to share my story, not for personal accolades but to shine a light on single mothers and mentors. This desire to give back and honor my journey would eventually be the start of the book you'd end up reading.

# BE A MAN, BE YOUR MAN

I just couldn't easily find the right moment and setting to conclude this book but right here, right now, I think this is the perfect time.

I write these final words as a grown man sitting at my kitchen table, the soft patter of my two children's feet echoing down the hall. It's early morning; my wife is still asleep, and our home is wrapped in a gentle quiet. In this stillness, I find myself reflecting on the journey from a fatherless boy to the father and husband I am today. I am a man raised by a woman, and now a man devoted to raising my own children with the same love and presence my mother showed me. If you were here with me now - just us two, sharing a pot of coffee - I'd tell you what's in my heart. This is the conversation I wish I could have with every friend, every son, every father out there about what manhood really means.

As you've read from my shared experiences, growing up without a father taught me that being a man is not about fitting some rigid mould. As a boy, I often searched for the shape of "manhood" in the dark, measuring myself against stereotypes I saw in movies or on the streets. I thought I had to be tough, unflinching, never shedding a tear. Society certainly sent me that message. But here's what I've learned sitting on the other side of childhood: *those messages were lies.*

Today I am a man who isn't afraid to kneel on the floor to play dolls with my daughter or to tell my son that it's okay to cry when he's hurt. I trade off cooking dinner with my wife and consider it as manly an act as bringing home a paycheck. *Yes, because real manhood is built on the pillars of integrity, responsibility, and love.*

## Challenging the Stereotypes of Manhood

Take a moment to think about how society often defines a "real man." From the time we are little, boys are bombarded with a very narrow script. Be strong. Be stoic. Never show vulnerability. Win at all costs. Don't back down. These ideas are reinforced in countless ways, from playground taunts ("stop crying like a girl") to cultural proverbs about men providing and women nurturing. By the time we reach adulthood, many of us have internalized the belief that to be a man, we must wear an armor of invincibility - an armor that hides our pain, our tenderness, our humanity.

Yet that armor comes at a tremendous cost.

It took me years to understand this, now it doesn't have to take you so long. As a young man, I, too, tried to live up to the cliché of the unfeeling tough guy. I remember when I was about 20, a close friend of mine died in an accident. At his funeral, I felt tears welling up, but I clamped down on them hard. I stood at the back, jaw tight, repeating to myself
the old mantra:

"Men don't cry."

I thought I was doing what was expected. But in truth, *I was robbing myself of the chance to heal.* I was distancing myself from the very emotions that make us human. I was not better for that stoicism; I was just alone in my grief.
Sadly, my experience isn't unique. As I grew older and more reflective, I started to notice how many men around me were suffering under the weight of these stereotypes. It's the colleague who jokes about needing a drink instead of admitting he's stressed. It's the friend who would rather rage or withdraw in silence than say "I'm hurt" or "I need help."
Modern research is now replete with evidence of how damaging these traditional notions of manhood can be. The American Psychological Association even issued guidelines warning that "traditional masculine ideology" marked by stoicism, suppression of emotions, and aggression can limit men's psychological development and well-being. In plain terms, when men are taught that talking about feelings or asking for help is a sign of weakness, they often end up suffering in silence.

We see the fallout in stark statistics. Around the world, men are disproportionately failing to cope in healthy ways. Consider mental health, for instance: men have a higher rate of suicide in country after country. Globally, men die by suicide at nearly twice the rate of women. One major reason, experts believe, is that men are far less likely to seek help or talk about what's hurting them. Traits of so-called "traditional masculinity" like masking distress and refusing to admit vulnerability have been linked to men's lower willingness to get therapy or medical care, more risk-taking behaviours, and higher levels of aggression. In short, men often "tough out" their pain until it harms them or those around them. When I first read these findings, I had to pause and let it sink in. It hit so close to home. I could have become one of those statistics, the silent sufferer, the man who cracks under pressure because he never learned how to ask for support.

The cultural script of stoicism doesn't just hurt men; it ripples outward and hurts women and children too. Imagine the father who's been told his whole life that caring for kids is "women's work." He might become the distant dad who never changes a diaper or attends a school play, depriving his children of his active love. Or think of the young man taught that dominance and control are marks of manhood. He might struggle to form equal, respectful partnerships with women. In the worst cases, this mindset contributes to abuse and violence.

There's well-established research linking adherence to hyper-traditional male norms with a greater propensity for domestic violence and sexual assault.

One Australian researcher put it bluntly:

*When boys are socialized to equate manhood with aggression and to view empathy or gentleness as "unmanly," it can turn lethal – not only for the men themselves (through accidents, fights, suicide) but also for the women and children in their lives*

That may sound harsh, but confronting these truths is part of how we heal. We can't fix what we don't face.

I want to be clear: being a man is not the problem; it's how we define being a man that is.

There's nothing wrong with strength, or courage, or ambition as these can be wonderful qualities. The issue is when we define strength as never showing softness, or courage as never asking for help, or ambition as a license to trample others. The issue is when half the range of human emotion is declared off-limits for men, when we tell boys that anger is acceptable but tears are not. For a long time, "maleness" has been a straitjacket that constrains half of our emotional spectrum. Society praises the stoic, "manly" men and sometimes sneers at the gentle, expressive ones. Yet if you ask me, the ability to express love, fear, or sorrow is just as much a mark of bravery as any physical feat.

Interestingly, everyday people are starting to recognize this imbalance. A 2024 Pew Research Center survey of Americans found that a majority of people comprising of men and women across political lines believe our society does not place enough value on qualities like being caring, affectionate, and emotionally open in men. Six in ten Americans said that we undervalue men who are kind and expressive, and many also felt that we place too much value on the old macho traits like being physically strong, aggressive, or a big risk-taker.

Think about that. Regular folks are saying, essentially, we've got it backwards. We're praising the wrong things in our sons and neglecting the traits that make good husbands, fathers, and citizens. This gives me hope that the tide is turning. Even as loud voices on cable TV or social media may rant about "manhood under attack," ordinary people can see that what's really under attack are the *men themselves* who are pressured on one side by outdated stereotypes and on the other side by the very real needs of their hearts that those stereotypes don't fulfil.

Our culture's narrow definition of manhood also polices men's relationships with each other. Many men struggle to form deep friendships because intimacy is seen as unmanly.

We tell boys to avoid any behavior that could be branded "soft." As a result, a lot of grown men have no one outside their romantic partner with whom they can share their soul. Loneliness among men is a growing issue; I've read studies suggesting men become lonelier as they age because they haven't built emotional connections, and indeed men often report fewer close friends than women do. I consider myself fortunate - being raised by a woman taught me early on the value of tenderness. My mother encouraged me to talk, to hug, to empathize. That has helped me keep and cultivate friendships with other men where we actually discuss our fears and dreams. But I know many guys who crave that kind of bond yet have no idea how to get it because it wasn't part of their model of manhood.

It's also important to say that these harmful myths about manhood rob society of good fathers. When a man believes that child-rearing is solely a woman's domain, or that being a dad is just about providing materially, he might become a physically or emotionally absent father. And when fathers vanish, families often pay a heavy price. I don't say this to discount the incredible job single mothers do (more on that soon), but rather to highlight a societal pattern.

In the United States, almost one in four children grows up without a father in the home, and the vast majority of single-parent households are headed by mothers. In fact, in America today there are roughly 7.3 million homes run by single mothers (versus about 2.5 million by single fathers). This isn't just an American phenomenon either. Globally, about 320 million children - 14% of all kids - live in single-parent households, and in more than 80% of those cases the single parent is the mother. These numbers represent countless evenings of one parent trying to do the job of two, countless children looking around for a dad who isn't there.

I was one of those kids.

And let me tell you, father absence leaves an imprint. My mother filled our home with love, and I owe everything good in my life to her sacrifices. But even she would agree that it was hard, that there were voids she alone couldn't completely fill. As a teen, I hungered for male guidance. I found some of it in teachers and coaches (and I thank God for those male mentors who stepped up), but many young men aren't so lucky. Statistically, children - especially boys - growing up without fathers are at higher risk for all sorts of challenges: dropping out of school, getting into trouble with the law, struggling with emotional regulation.

One extensive Harvard study found that boys from low-income single-parent families were significantly less likely to finish school or avoid unemployment than their peers in two-parent homes and notably, even less likely than their sisters in the same household.
The researchers suggested that fatherless boys in tough neighbourhoods often lack the male role models and sense of structure that might otherwise steer them away from destructive paths. One report starkly noted, youths from father-absent homes face higher odds of poverty and even an almost threefold greater risk of involvement in crime like gun violence and drug trafficking.

None of this is to say that a child raised by a single mother is doomed; absolutely not. If anything, these facts should shine a light on how heroic single parents are, and how much more support society ought to give them and their kids. When I cite those sobering statistics, I'm calling out a cultural failure, not a personal one. The failure is on us men - and on societal institutions - for not doing better by our children. The way I see it, every absent father is a man who, somewhere along the way, didn't grasp what his true role could be. Maybe he never had a father to show him. Maybe he was never taught the deeper definition of manhood that includes being a nurturer. Or maybe economic and social barriers drove him away. Regardless, the result is millions of women and children carrying burdens that should have been shared. As a society, we simply must do better to support and encourage responsible, loving fatherhood.

## A New Vision of Manhood: Presence, Integrity, Empathy

So what does a healthier, value-based version of manhood look like? Over the years, I've pieced together an answer from my experiences, from watching other men I admire, and from diving into research and conversations. I'd distill it into a few core principles:

*presence, integrity, empathy, and love.* To me, these qualities are the bedrock of real masculinity, and they are entirely compatible with strength and leadership. In fact, I'd argue they enhance those traditional virtues.

**Presence** is first. By presence, I mean being there in every sense of the word. A real man shows up for his children, his partner, his friends, his community. He doesn't check out when life gets hard; he leans in. I think of presence as the opposite of abdication. My father abdicated his role, leaving my mother and me on our own. I vowed never to do the same. Now, as a father, presence means that if my daughter has a school recital, I'm in the front row cheering. If my son wakes up from a nightmare, I'm by his bedside reassuring him that he's safe. Presence also means emotional availability. My kids know that *Daddy will listen* to them whether they're upset or excited or confused and not dismiss their feelings. This is something many of us didn't get from our dads, but we can change that pattern.

Research shows that such fatherly involvement yields incredible benefits. Engaged fathers contribute to kids' higher self-esteem, better academic outcomes, and healthier social behavior. Even something as simple as a dad reading bedtime stories or tossing a ball in the yard can positively affect a child's cognitive development and confidence. And the benefits extend beyond the kids as mothers benefit, too, when fathers are truly coparenting.

Studies have found that moms experience significantly less stress and lower rates of depression when the father is an active participant in parenting. I saw this in my own marriage - when our first baby was born, I made it a point to do my share of midnight feedings and diaper changes. Not only did this give my wife much-needed rest, but it also bonded me with my daughter from day one. Presence is a gift that keeps giving.

Next comes **integrity** and **responsibility**. These might sound like old-fashioned concepts, but they never go out of style. Integrity means your word matters - you do what you say you'll do, you stand up for what you believe is right, and you live in alignment with your values. A man of integrity doesn't abandon his responsibilities when they become inconvenient. Responsibility, in this context, means owning your duties as a father, a partner, a citizen. It means *providing* in the broadest sense: not just financially, but providing guidance, support, and accountability. One of the best pieces of advice I ever got was from a mentor who told me,

*"Being a father is about showing up consistently.*
*Anyone can make a baby, but a man of character*
*raises his children every single day."*

We need more of that ethos. If you bring a child into this world, it is your sacred responsibility to be there for them. Period. That doesn't mean you won't make mistakes - you will (I know I have). But integrity means you own up to those mistakes, you apologize when needed, and you keep striving to be better.

Consider the ripple effects if more men embraced this. For one, we'd break those generational cycles of abandonment. There's evidence that boys who grow up with absent fathers are more likely to become absent fathers themselves (and similarly, girls who grow up fatherless often end up with partners who repeat the pattern). I was painfully aware of that statistic when I became a dad; it haunted me as a cautionary tale. But standing here now, I also see it as inspiration: by choosing to be a present, responsible father, I'm not only doing right by my kids, I'm also rewriting my family legacy. I've severed the chain that linked my father and me. My son and daughter will never doubt whether their dad loves them or whether he'll stick around. They know I'm here, always. And maybe one day, when my son has children of his own, he'll draw on the model I provided. That's how we slowly, family by family, reshape what fatherhood and manhood mean for the next generation.

**Empathy** and **emotional courage** are another pillar of healthy masculinity. It takes strength to feel deeply and to care deeply. Don't let anyone tell you otherwise. In fact, think of the bravest men in history or in your life - the ones truly worth admiring. Weren't they men who showed compassion, who fought for others, who were unafraid to wear their heart on their sleeve when it counted? We need to raise boys who are as comfortable saying "I care" as they are saying "I'm strong." The two are not mutually exclusive.

Cultivating empathy in men also directly addresses some of the societal harms we discussed earlier. A man who can empathize with others is less likely to be violent or cruel.

He's more likely to be a supportive partner and an involved parent. There's a beautiful saying I once heard: *"Raise boys who will cry, and you won't have to raise boys who will make others cry."* It struck me because it flips the script. It suggests that by allowing boys their full emotional range, we actually raise kinder, better men. Modern psychology backs this up: when men are allowed and encouraged to be emotionally literate, they tend to have healthier relationships and cause less harm. One Australian mental health expert noted that if boys are socialized to always avoid showing weakness or dependency, it later stunts them in friendships, marriages, and parenting. On the flip side, teaching boys empathy and emotional honesty lays a foundation for them to become men who communicate, who nurture, and who resolve conflicts without resorting to fists or fury.

Another key aspect of redefining manhood is respect for others as equals. Traditional machismo often positioned men above women - "the king of the castle" mentality. We must finally put that to rest. A real man does not fear a woman's strength or success; he celebrates it. In my marriage, I see my wife as my partner in every sense. There's no "who's the boss" in our home. We both are, in different arenas. Some days she leads, some days I do, often we lead side by side. Early in our marriage, an acquaintance made a snide joke to me, saying I was "whipped" because I openly supported my wife's career ambitions and did a lot of the cooking. I laughed it off, but it revealed a mindset that's sadly common: the notion that a man loses status if he treats a woman as an equal or - heaven forbid - takes on traditionally "feminine" chores. This thinking is toxic and absurd.

My response is simple: *a confident man isn't diminished by a woman's shine; he's enhanced by it.* I am a better man because I uplift the women in my life rather than compete with them or try to control them. That applies not only to my wife but also to my daughter, my female colleagues, friends, and so on. One day my daughter will choose a partner; I want her to know beyond doubt that she deserves respect and true partnership, because she saw her father model it.

## A Conversation Across Generations and Cultures

The beautiful thing about redefining manhood is that it's not just a personal journey but a collective one. And it's happening across generations and cultures. Over the past few years, I've had the privilege of speaking with men from various walks of life about these issues. I've chatted with elders in my community, young men just starting out, and peers my own age. The specifics of our experiences differ, but I kept hearing a common theme: *the old model of manhood isn't fitting right anymore. It's like a suit that's two sizes too small and people are ready to tailor a new one.*

Speaking of community, I think about broader social influences like schools, media, workplaces, places of worship, and the role they play in shaping or reshaping our idea of manhood. We all consume the narratives that these institutions put out. I've noticed more children's TV shows nowadays featuring caring, sensitive dad characters (an encouraging sign!). Some schools have started programs to teach boys emotional skills and consent and cooperation from a young age. Workplaces are offering paternity leave and encouraging fathers to take it, which sends a message that a dad's place can indeed be in the home, bonding with a newborn. These are subtle but powerful shifts. For example, I recently read a statistic that in the U.S., more fathers are taking advantage of parental leave than ever before - still a minority, but the numbers are rising annually. Each father who takes that leave is quietly asserting: my value isn't only at the office, it's also right here cradling my child at 3 AM. Each employer that normalizes this is helping carve a new norm.

There's also movement in the faith community. As a person of faith myself, I recall hearing mostly about the man as the "head of the household" in church growing up. Now, I've attended men's retreats where the talk is about servant leadership and emotional integrity where men are encouraged to confess their fears and struggles to one another. In one such retreat, I witnessed a burly, tattooed former marine break down and weep as he talked about wanting to reconcile with his estranged son. Instead of anyone ridiculing him, all the other men including myself gave all the support we could. It was such a human moment. We were just a bunch of fathers and sons, wanting to be better, trying to heal. Moments like that give me faith that across communities, we can foster a new kind of masculinity that's as compassionate as it is strong.

## A Call to Action: Redefining Manhood Together

So where do we go from here? It's all well and good to talk about these ideals, but change has to happen on multiple levels: personal, cultural, institutional. *Each of us has a role.*

**To the men reading this:** I speak to you first as a brother. Whether you're 16 or 60, it's never too early or too late to rethink what it means to be a man. Take a hard look at the ideas you were taught. Which ones serve you and those you love, and which ones don't? Give yourself permission to break out of the old mould. If you have children, especially sons, know that they are watching you to learn how to be. Model the behavior you wish you'd learned. Show them that a man can be affectionate, that a man can apologize, that a man can cry and it doesn't diminish his strength one bit. And if you have daughters, model the kind of man you'd want them to be around - respectful, supportive, and empathetic.

Challenge yourself in small ways: call up a friend just to talk about life beyond sports or work; change a diaper or make a meal if you usually don't; the next time you're struggling emotionally, consider talking to someone or even a counsellor instead of bottling it up.

These may seem like personal actions, but they are quietly revolutionary. They

chip away at the old paradigm and build a new one. Importantly, hold other men accountable too, but with compassion. If a buddy makes a misogynistic joke or belittles his wife, don't laugh it off but speak up. Sometimes all it takes is one man saying "Not cool, man. We don't do that," to make others reconsider their behavior. Conversely, if you see a fellow man being brave in his vulnerability or doing the right thing, encourage it. We men often rag on each other for sport, but let's start *praising each other for growth and goodness.*
Make it "cool" to be a good guy.

I also urge you not to be afraid of seeking help. Too many men wait until they are at a breaking point like marriage on the rocks, substance addiction, or mental health crisis before they consider therapy or joining a support group or even opening up to a friend. I've been there, wrestling alone with anxiety and the traumas of my youth. It was humbling to admit I needed counselling to process some of my pain. But doing so changed my life; it made me a better father and husband, and frankly a happier human being. If you're in a dark place, please reach out; it could be to a professional, a mentor, a faith leader, anyone you trust. There is no shame in needing others. In fact, it's profoundly human and, I'd argue, profoundly masculine in the healthiest sense. The data is clear that when men forego help, the results can be tragic; recall that men often have lower diagnosed depression rates but higher suicide rates, partly because they aren't getting help in time. Don't be a statistic; be the man who had the courage to take the lifeline.

**To the women reading this:** You might be a mother, a sister, a wife, a girlfriend, a friend, a daughter. You have a stake in this too, and a tremendous influence. I want to acknowledge and thank the women like you, because without my mother and a few strong women mentors, I wouldn't be half the man I am. Continue to encourage the men in your life to open up and be themselves. If you're raising a son, know that you absolutely can raise him into a good man even if a father figure is absent. The love, structure, and values you impart will be his foundation. Surround him with positive male role models in family or community if you can - coaches, teachers, uncles, family friends - because it does help to see examples of honorable men. But even if those are scarce, your influence is immeasurable. Teach him empathy, respect, self-discipline, and he will carry those into manhood. I often think of how my mother taught me "gentlemanliness" not by demanding I be tough, but by demanding I be thoughtful in things like saying "please" and "thank you," looking people in the eye, standing up for the vulnerable. Those lessons are the essence of being a good man.

**To wives and partners:** challenge us men when we retreat behind emotional walls. Invite us to share. Many of us truly want to, but decades of conditioning make us hesitant.
My wife has this way of patiently waiting me out when I give the classic "I'm fine" response even though she can see I'm not. She'll sit with me, sometimes

in silence, sometimes gently saying, "It's okay, I'm here whenever you want to talk." That simple presence can crack open the dam. And when we do open up, receive us without judgment. For example, if your husband or boyfriend cries in front of you for the first time, realize what a huge step that is for him. Don't recoil; hold him. Show him that you still respect and love him just the same (and even more). That affirmation is powerful. Don't conform! Also, keep expecting more from us in terms of partnership at home and with children. Sometimes we slack because society has allowed us to. But when you expect and believe that we are capable of being equal caregivers and homemakers, it pushes us to rise to the occasion. I firmly believe men should do an equal share of the nurturing and household work, and many of us were never really taught how. So, teach us, involve us, insist on it. We'll all be better for it.

**To communities, institutions, and leaders:** there is much you can do to support this redefinition of manhood. Education is key so why not incorporate soial-emotional learning that is tailored to boys' development in school curricula? Encourage boys to read books and watch films that expand their view of masculinity (I think every teenage boy should read something like *"Between the World and Me" or "The Boy Crisis"* or watch positive role models in media). Faith communities can preach and model inclusive, loving manhood rather than domineering patriarchy. Workplaces can create cultures that respect work-life balance for men as well as women - offering parental leave, not penalizing dads for taking time for family, maybe even something as simple as encouraging men to be open about family commitments. The government and nonprofits can invest in mentorship programs. I was part of a mentorship initiative that paired fatherless teen boys with adult male mentors, and I saw lives changed one Saturday afternoon at a time - whether it was mentors teaching these boys how to fix a car or just taking them out for pizza and a heart-to-heart talk. Expanding such programs, especially in high-risk communities, can fill critical gaps. Also, let's support mental health resources geared toward men. Removing the stigma through public awareness campaigns can make it more acceptable for a man to attend a support group or therapy. Imagine seeing a billboard with a tough-looking guy and the words: "It takes a real man to ask for help - Call 800-XXX-XXXX." We need those messages out there to counteract the years of the opposite.

Media and entertainment also have a responsibility. Storytellers, please give us more nuanced portraits of men. Show the hero who saves the day and goes to therapy for his PTSD. Show the single dad who isn't just comedic relief but is competent and caring. Show teenage boys who solve conflicts with dialogue and compassion, not just fists. Pop culture is a powerful teacher; it taught generations of boys that violence and stoicism were cool, now it can teach that empathy and collaboration are cool too. And to be fair, I have seen progress here - from Mr. Rogers long ago to modern kids' cartoons where male characters talk about feelings. Keep it up, because those images sink in.

Lastly, as a society, we must tackle the underlying issues that make healthy family life hard. Poverty, lack of education, mass incarceration, substance abuse are all factors that can strip away fathers from homes and destabilize young men's futures. It's beyond the scope of this conclusion to delve deeply into those, but they can't be ignored. If we want more present fathers, we need to create conditions that allow men to be present: jobs that pay a living wage, criminal justice reform, community support for families in need, and so on.

# A Tribute to Single Mothers - and to the Village that Raises a Man

Before I close, I must pay tribute to the true heroes of my story and of so many stories like mine: **single mothers**. To any single mother reading this, I want you to know that you are seen, you are respected, and you are loved. You are doing one of the hardest jobs on the planet, and doing it without the built-in support system that a partner provides. The world often doesn't give you enough credit. There were times my mother felt invisible, working two jobs, coming home exhausted to help me with homework, stretching every dollar, dealing with the quiet ache of loneliness after I went to bed. Society can be harsh on single moms, blaming them for struggles that are usually the fallout of some man's irresponsibility or larger social failures. Yet, you persevere. Studies acknowledge that single mothers (and fathers) face immense challenges - economic hardships, social stigma, personal strain - but those studies rarely capture the intangible superpowers you develop: resilience, resourcefulness, an ocean-deep well of love.

My mother used to say, "I'm both mother and father to you," and in many ways she was. She taught me how to shave and how to pray. She took me to football practice and cheered the loudest, then somehow found time to cook a pot of chili for the team fundraiser. She did the work of two, and while I know it wore her down, she raised me to feel like I never lacked for anything essential. How do you even say thank you for that?

This book may be about becoming a man, but it is equally about the woman who made that possible. Mom, if you're reading, this is my eternal thank you. You showed me that love has no gender - you gave me a mother's tenderness and a father's discipline in equal measure. You also never spoke ill of my father in front of me, even though he likely deserved it. Instead, you focused on what we had. You told me, "James, you can be anything a man should be - you are strong, you are kind, and you are my son." In doing so, you planted the seed in me that has now grown into the convictions I've shared here. I owe my vision of healthy manhood largely to you.

And to all the single mothers: your sons and daughters may become the next generation of amazing men and women precisely because of your influence. If I have any right to give advice, I'd say this: don't let anyone convince you that you can't raise a man. You absolutely can. Surround yourself and your children with a supportive community. Take care of your mental health (you deserve to not run yourself into the ground - I know it's easier said than done, but remember you can't pour from an empty cup). Accept help when offered; it's not a sign of failure but of community. And know that many of us out here admire you deeply. I, for one, will spend my life advocating for more support for single parents from better childcare options to equitable pay and family leave policies, because no one who is doing the incredible work of raising a child alone should have to do it without a safety net.

I also want to acknowledge the broader "villages" that often step in to raise fatherless children. In my life, that village included a grandfather who imparted wisdom in his gentle way, a coach who taught me about perseverance, a teacher who encouraged my writing, church members who lent us a hand when times were tight, and even peers who shared their dads with me on weekends. If you're part of that village for someone, if you mentor a youth, or you're an uncle who spends extra time with a nephew, or a family friend who invites the single-parent family over for holidays, please know what a profound impact you have. Sometimes a child only needs one adult to believe in them for them to start believing in themselves. Be that person if you can. I've tried to pay forward the blessings I received by mentoring young men in my community, and it's one of the most rewarding aspects of my life.

In all, *let's redefine manhood together, in our homes, in our hearts, and in our culture.*

Let's take all that is good from our fathers' and grandfathers' eras like the loyalty, the sense of duty, the bravery, and merge it with a new openness, a new compassion that the future desperately needs. We owe it not just to ourselves, but to our sons and daughters.

I often think about the kind of world my children will inherit. My daughter should grow up expecting respect and partnership from the men in her life, and never doubting her equal worth. My son should grow up free to be gentle or bold, artistic or athletic, or all of those at once, without his identity as a "man" ever being questioned. They both should grow up in a society where men are allies and caregivers and peacemakers as much as they are anything else.

To get there, it starts with conversations like the one we're virtually having now. It starts with one man deciding to be different, one woman encouraging a change, one community supporting a new norm. It's already happening, and you and I can be part of pushing that momentum forward. Think of this not as the end of my memoir, but as the beginning of a movement - or at least, the continuation of one that's been a long time coming.

Thank you for listening to my story and my reflections. If you're a man who, like me, was raised by a single mother (or otherwise lacked a father figure), I especially want you to take heart. We are not anomalies; we are proof that love makes families, not just biology.

And we have a unique role to play in reshaping manhood, because we've seen up close that strength and tenderness are not opposites - our mothers showed us both. Carry that lesson with you. Live it, and teach it to those around you.

As I finish writing, the sun is higher and I can hear my kids giggling about something, probably coaxing their mom to make pancakes. In a minute, I'll join them. That is where manhood lives for me now - in those small, sweet moments of being a dad and a husband. Not in any accolades or macho conquests, but in the simple fulfilment of being present and full of love. My journey to manhood, raised by a woman, has come full circle: I am the man I am because a strong woman taught me how to love.

Consider this conclusion a letter from that boy I once was; the boy with a hole in his heart where his father should've been, the boy who sat with his mother as a child and ate pancakes for breakfast with such powerful assurance that everything was alright, the boy who had a mother that believed in him regardless of the odds and of the greater tendencies that I wasn't going to grow to be the man she wished me to be but instead to be a product of societal condemnation. This is to the man I became, and to anyone who's ever wondered what it really means to "be a man." We have the power to define it for ourselves.

So let's do it. It starts with each of us, and it starts now.

# References

1. **Black Dog Institute.** (2014). Report on men's psychological distress and suicidal behavior. (Findings cited in Willis, 2019, ABC News) v

2. **Chamie, J.** (2016, October 15). 320 Million Children in Single-Parent Families. Global Issues/Inter Press Service. Retrieved from https://www.globalissues.org/news/2016/10/15/22568

3. **Flood, M.** (2019). In O. Willis, Traditional masculinity and men's mental health [Interview]. Australian Psychological Society discussion on APA Guidelines.

4. **Horowitz, J. M., & Parker, K.** (2024, October 17). How Americans see men and masculinity. Pew Research Center. Retrieved from https://www.pewresearch.org/social-trends/2024/10/17/how-americans-see-men-and-masculinity/

5. **Kramer, S. (2019, December 12).** U.S. has world's highest rate of children living in single-parent households. Pew Research Center. Retrieved from https://www.pewresearch.org/short-reads/2019/12/12/u-s-children-more-likely-than-children-in-other-countries-to-live-with-just-one-parent/

6. **National Fatherhood Initiative.** (n.d.). Father Absence Statistics. Retrieved 2025, October 4, from https://www.fatherhood.org/father-absence-statistic

7. **Sawhill, I. V.** (2016, February 9). Boys need fathers, but don't forget about the girls. Brookings Institution. Retrieved from https://www.brookings.edu/articles/boys-need-fathers-but-dont-forget-about-the-girls/

8. **U.S. Census Bureau.** (2024, March 21). National Single Parent Day: March 21, 2024 (Facts for Features). Retrieved from https://www.census.gov/newsroom/stories/single-parent-day.html

9. **Willis, O. (2019, February 4).** "Traditional masculinity" and mental health: Experts call for gendered approach to treatment. ABC News (Australia). Retrieved from https://www.abc.net.au/news/health/2019-02-05/mens-mental-health-masculinity-gendered-psychology-guide-lines/10768294

10. **World Health Organization.** (2019, April 4). Uneven access to health services drives life expectancy gaps: WHO [Press release]. Retrieved from https://www.who.int/news/item/04-04-2019-uneven-access-to-health-ser-vices drives-life-expectancy-gaps-who